Library of
Davidson College

OECD

MONETARY STUDIES SERIES

MONETARY TARGETS
AND
INFLATION CONTROL

1979

332.41
068m

The Organisation for Economic Co-operation and Development (OECD) was set up under a Convention signed in Paris on 14th December 1960, which provides that the OECD shall promote policies designed:
- to achieve the highest sustainable economic growth and employment and a rising standard of living in Member countries, while maintaining financial stability, and thus to contribute to the development of the world economy;
- to contribute to sound economic expansion in Member as well as non-member countries in the process of economic development;
- to contribute to the expansion of world trade on a multilateral, non-discriminatory basis in accordance with international obligations.

The Members of OECD are Australia, Austria, Belgium, Canada, Denmark, Finland, France, the Federal Republic of Germany, Greece, Iceland, Ireland, Italy, Japan, Luxembourg, the Netherlands, New Zealand, Norway, Portugal, Spain, Sweden, Switzerland, Turkey, the United Kingdom and the United States.

© OECD, 1979
Queries concerning permissions or translation rights should be addressed to:
Director of Information, OECD
2, rue André-Pascal, 75775 PARIS CEDEX 16, France.

CONTENTS

Foreword		5
Introduction		7
Part I.	CONCEPTUAL AND QUANTITATIVE ASPECTS OF MONETARY TARGETING	17
	A. The Rationale for Target-Oriented Monetary Management	17
	Neo-Keynesian and portfolio-balance modelling	18
	Neo-Classical "rationalism"	19
	Monetarism	19
	Global monetarism	20
	B. Recent Tendencies in Official Thinking	20
	C. Policy-Making under Uncertainty	21
	Rules versus discretion	21
	"Optimal" economic control	22
	D. Criteria for Choosing among Aggregates	24
	Controllability	24
	Predictability of effects	25
Part II.	EXPERIENCE WITH MONETARY TARGETING	29
	United States	29
	Japan	36
	Germany	38
	France	45
	United Kingdom	48
	Italy	52
	Canada	57
Part III.	BENEFIT AND COST OF MONETARY TARGETING	63
	A. Monetary Performance	63
	B. Inflation Control and External Equilibrium	64
	C. Policy Coordination	66
	Package deals	66
	Budget financing	67
	Exchange rate constraints	67
	D. Opportunity Costs for Output and Employment	68
	Concluding Remarks	69
Annex I.	Country Charts	71
Annex II.	The Experience of Smaller Open Economies	87
Annex III.	Selected Bibliography	95

TABLES

Main Text

1.	Transition to Published Monetary Targets	7
2.	Official Liquidity Creation	11
3.	Projected and Actual Rates of Monetary Growth	13
4.	Income Velocity in Major OECD Countries, 1965-1977	26
5.	Stability Properties of Demand for Money Functions in Major OECD Countries	27
6.	German Interbank Rates, 1973-1974	39
7.	Germany: Central Bank Money Stock and its Determinants	41
8.	Recent Developments in Monetary Aggregates in Germany	44
9.	Italy: Monetary Aggregates and Nominal Product	56
10.	Economic Target Variables	65

Annex

A.	Switzerland: Monetary Aggregates, Output and Prices	90
B.	Belgium: Selected Financial and General Economic Indicators	91
C.	Denmark: Selected Financial and General Economic Indicators	93

CHARTS

Main Text

1.	The Transmission Process of Monetary Policy	8-9
2.	Monetary Growth and Prices in the OECD area, 1965-1975	10
3.	Federal Reserve Target-Setting and Implementation	32
4.	Monetary Management and Interest Rate Trends: United States	34
5.	Monetary Management and Interest Rate Trends: Germany	42
6.	Monetary Management and Interest Rate Trends: France	47
7.	Monetary Management and Interest Rate Trends: United Kingdom	51
8.	Total Domestic Credit and Treasury Financing in Italy	55
9.	Monetary Management and Interest Rate Trends: Canada	60

Annex

A.	General Economic Indicators	72
B.	Policy Indicators	73
C.	Monetary Management and Interest Rate Trends: Switzerland	89

Key to Symbols

.. not available.
— nil or negligible.
Q1, Q4 calendar quarters.

FOREWORD

The OECD Monetary Studies were initiated in the early 1970s at the request of the Economic Policy Committee. Each of the first five volumes analysed monetary structures and policies in a selected OECD country.[1] The series was then supplemented by a comparative survey: *The Role of Monetary Policy in Demand Management — The Experience of Six Major Countries* (1975). The studies were undertaken in response to the need for detailed analysis of the conduct and influence of monetary policy, since its use in controlling aggregate demand had increased, and since international capital movements — through their domestic monetary effects — impinged with increasing frequency on policy actions in individual countries.

The present report updates and expands the 1975 comparative study, reviewing monetary experience in the seven largest OECD countries, as well as in selected smaller ones, over the period 1974-1978. It takes account of the significant evolution of monetary management which has occurred — notably in relation to the rapid acceleration of inflation during the present decade. Specifically, the widespread adoption of official guidelines for the growth of monetary and credit aggregates has become of great interest in the context of inflation control.

This new survey has been prepared by the Monetary and Fiscal Policy Division of the Economics and Statistics Department. Its preliminary versions were discussed at meetings of Working Party No. 4 of the Economic Policy Committee as part of its work on policies against inflation, and were further examined by a group of official monetary experts. The present volume is published under the responsibility of the Secretary-General. The views expressed therein are those of the authors and do not necessarily represent those of the OECD or its Member governments.

---

1. See *Monetary Policy in Japan* (1972); *Monetary Policy in Italy* (1973); *Monetary Policy in Germany* (1973); *Monetary Policy in the United States* (1974); *Monetary Policy in France* (1974).

INTRODUCTION

A growing number of central banks in OECD Member countries have begun to chart their policies in the framework of intermediate quantitative monetary objectives in recent years. Target growth rates or projections for the money stock or domestic credit aggregates in various definitions are now published in advance in the seven larger OECD countries. Similar practices are being followed in *Australia,* the *Netherlands, Spain* and *Switzerland* (Table 1). Other countries have shown reluctance to commit themselves to monetary aggregate objectives, and in some cases—notably in *Austria, Belgium* and *Scandinavian* countries—the authorities have expressed profound scepticism as to the virtues of monetary "targetry" in general, its relevance for dependent open economies, or the desirability of monetary "norms" in their specific national socio-economic context.

Several factors seem to have combined to strengthen treasuries' and central banks' inclination to adopt quantitative policy approaches—even though they

Table 1. TRANSITION TO PUBLISHED MONETARY TARGETS

Country	Aggregate	Projection period	Target[a]
Italy	Total domestic credit	March 1974 - March 1975	Lit. 21,800 billion
Germany	Central bank money stock	End-1974 - End 1975	8
Switzerland	M1	December 1974 - December 1975	6
Spain	M3	January-June 1975	18[b]
United States	M1 M2 M3	March 1975 - March 1976	5-7½ 8½- 10½ 10-12
Canada	M1	1975QII - 1976QII	10-15
United Kingdom	M3	Fiscal year ending April 1977	12
Australia	M3	July 1976 - June 1977	10-12[c]
France	M2	December 1976 - December 1977	12½
Netherlands	M2/Net national income[d]	End-1976 to 1977-80	37[b]
Japan	M2	Third quarter 1978	11-12[e]

a) Absolute or percentage increase or limit for target variable over first period for which monetary objective was published.
b) Progressively declining.
c) Guideline.
d) Domestic liquidity ratio.
e) Forecast.
Source: OECD Secretariat.

Chart 1. THE TRANSMIS

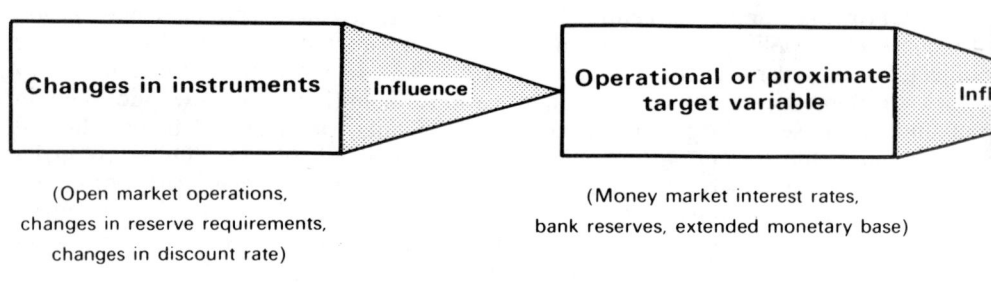

(Open market operations, changes in reserve requirements, changes in discount rate)

(Money market interest rates, bank reserves, extended monetary base)

Note: This presentation is based on a simplified approach of the monetary transmission process as described in "Towards Full E of feedback effects on instrumental variables.

involve an unusual degree of exposure to public debate and criticism—and the weight of those influences has varied among countries and over time. The transition to monetary targeting can be traced back to the 1960s, although central banks appear to have been particularly heavily influenced by the fairly general inflation experience of the present decade and the new exchange rate situation after 1973. The postwar "monetarist challenge" and the subsequent "neo-Keynesian" rebuttal instilled or reawakened wider interest in the macroeconomic role of money, the possible control function of the money stock, and "rules" for "steady" monetary growth. A protracted and still continuing expert debate on the structure of the monetary control problem led to a more rigorous perception of the transmission mechanism of monetary policy and pointed to a potentially competing role of market interest rates and monetary aggregates as the most efficient indicators or intermediate policy objectives (Chart 1).[1] Central banks actively participated in the discussion, and their monetary operating techniques began to show signs of changing emphasis.

Between the mid-1960s and the mid-1970s there was thus a gradual decline in preoccupation with interest rates in policy formulation and implementation that coincided with an increased attention to the behaviour of monetary and credit aggregates as an intermediate policy guide. Apart from changes in central banking doctrine, these shifts in policy attitudes were, to varying degrees, conditioned also by typical experiences and obstacles which monetary authorities

1. It is important in this context to distinguish the practice of *controlling* directly bank credit expansion from that of monetary targeting. The former is, in terms of Chart 1, a form of instrument, while money and credit aggregates are considered to be intermediate targets. The practical use of each concept is considered in more depth in Part II.

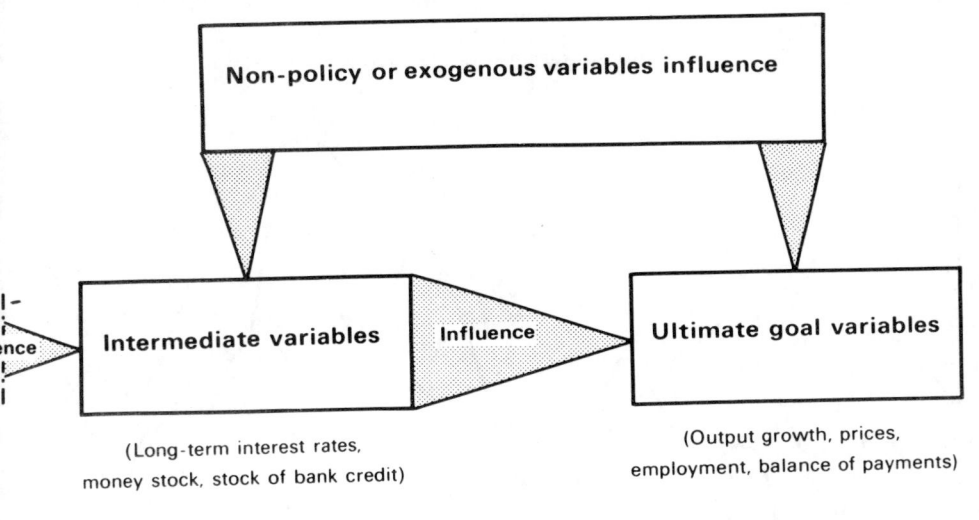

encountered in day-to-day policy-making. The doubling of the inflation rate to 5 per cent and more in the OECD area in 1969-1970 and its subsequent advance to double-digit levels in 1974-1975 were preceded or accompanied by rapidly accelerating rates of monetary expansion in major Member countries (Chart 2). Easy monetary conditions contributed to general excess demand, overstimulation of the housing market, commodity and property speculation, and unrestrained cost inflation.

Efficient maintenance of monetary control was hampered during this period for a variety of reasons which all pointed to an apparent need for closer observation of monetary aggregates and cast doubt on the reliability of market interest rates as a dominant policy guide:

— Market interest rates—unless administered directly by the authorities as in *Japan*—tend to move spontaneously up and down with recovery and recession periods. The underlying mechanism is rarely well understood by the public, which tends to associate rising interest rates generally with a tighter policy posture. Central banks may therefore have been reluctant to initiate restrictive action in time.

— By overtly aiming at higher market interest rates, the monetary authorities were faced with the necessity to weaken the position of highly interest-sensitive sectors of the economy. In particular in the *United States* and, to a lesser extent, in the *United Kingdom*, where rising shorter-term market interest rates cut down the growth of deposits and so quickly eroded the lending capacity of housing finance institutions, concerns about the housing sector or the viability of thrift institutions limited the flexibility of monetary management.

— Underprediction of the acceleration of inflation and of the gradual disappearance of "money illusion" led to abnormally depressed "real"

Chart 2. MONETARY GROWTH AND PRICES IN THE OECD, AREA, 1965-1975

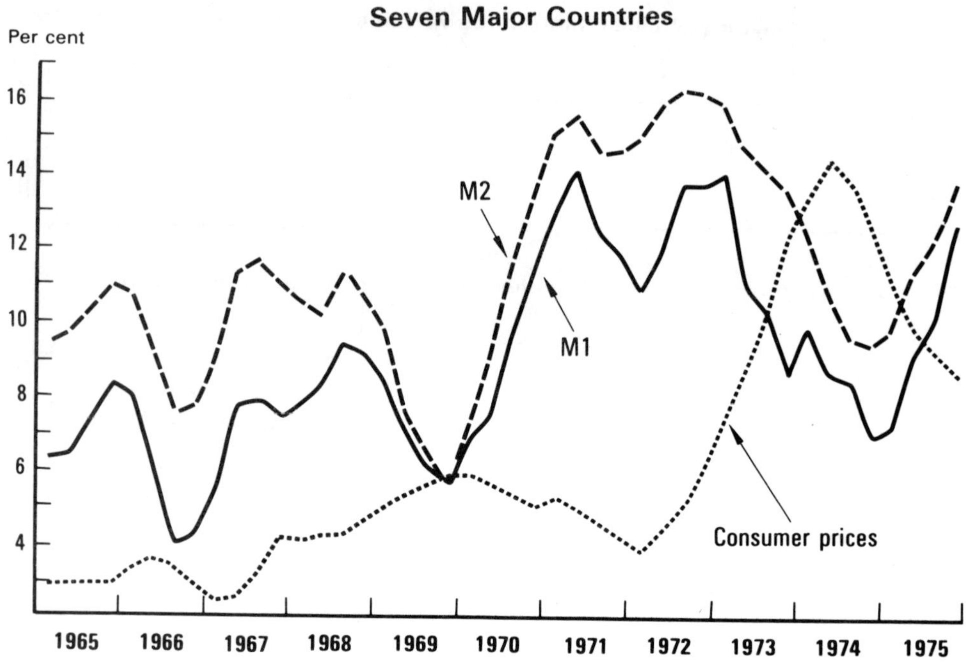

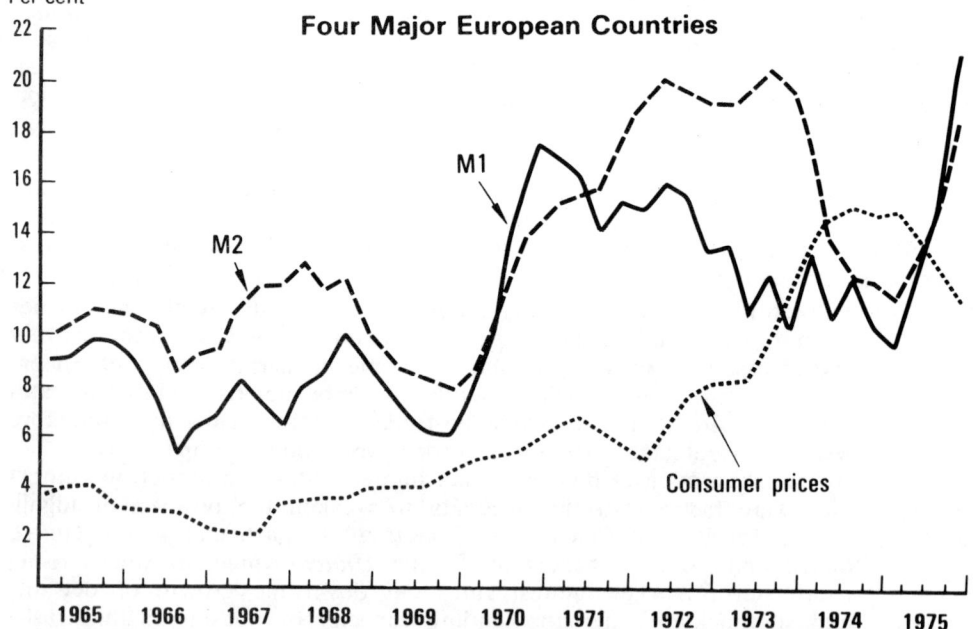

Note: Movements in money supply (seasonally adjusted) and consumer prices are shown as quarter-on-quarter percentage changes at annual rates, smoothed by three quarter moving averages. Money supply data are calculated at constant 4th quarter 1970 dollar rates. Consumer price indices are weighted by 1970 private consumption figures.

market interest rates during the boom period of the early 1970s. For the first time in a decade, the GNP-weighted "OECD bond rate" fell below the rise in the area's consumer prices towards the end of 1972.

— Exchange market intervention during the terminal stages of the Bretton-Woods system in 1970-1973 led to annual increases in world exchange reserves between 15 and 45 per cent (Table 2). These developments weakened the external constraints on expansionary monetary management perceived by governments in reserve accumulating countries; and monetary control in some of them was undermined due to the concomitant creation of domestic excess liquidity which the public hardly viewed as a serious matter for concern.

Table 2. OFFICIAL LIQUIDITY CREATION
$ billion

	Amounts outstanding: end of period		
	1969	1973	1975
Total[a]	78.4	183.7	227.4
Composition:			
SDRs	—	10.6	10.3
Gold	39.1	43.0	41.6
Reserve position in the Fund	6.7	7.4	14.8
Currency assets	32.6	122.6	160.8
Distribution:			
OECD countries	60.9	136.6	137.2
Oil-exporting countries	4.2	14.5	56.5
Non-oil developing countries	10.9	27.5	29.6
Others	2.4	5.0	4.0

Note: Detail may not add due to rounding.
a) The percentage rate of growth of international liquidity was:
1969	1970	1971	1972	1973	1974	1975
0.8	18.9	43.5	19.2	15.2	20.0	3.1

Source: OECD Secretariat.

"Overshooting" of monetary management in a contractionary direction must also be regarded as characteristic of the earlier period, partly reflecting the short-run orientation of central banks' traditional operating strategy. Important examples were the 1966 and 1969 "credit crunches" in the *United States* and the first postwar recession in *Germany* in 1966-1967. The unexpected depth of the world economic recession after the 1973-1974 oil crisis, to which monetary and a complex of other factors contributed, provided the most recent case in point. Policy-controlled short-term money market rates climbed to historic peak levels in many OECD countries in the second half of 1974, while monetary growth—both nominal and "real"—was sharply decelerating, and the world economy was clearly heading into recession. All these events contributed to the growing disenchantment with discretionary monetary "fine tuning" and helped prepare the ground for innovative experiments geared to a medium-term time horizon in the field of monetary management.

The transition to explicit target-constrained monetary management and the official announcement of longer-term objectives for money and credit aggregates during the mid-1970s thus continued already discernible tendencies in monetary policy-making. It is interesting to note that, in a number of countries, governments or parliaments, rather than central banks, took the initiative of advocating or suggesting the public announcement of quantitative monetary objectives. In response, the monetary authorities have generally appreciated and availed themselves of the potential persuasive influence on public opinion of quantified credit policy statements. In the stronger economies, in which balance of payments concerns did not play a role, the practice of publishing monetary objectives was closely associated with domestic stabilisation efforts provoked by the upsurge in prices and the recession during the years 1974-1975 (*United States, Germany, Switzerland*). In other larger economies, which to varying degrees were confronted with recurrent balance of payments difficulties, the adoption of quantitative intermediate objectives typically responded both to domestic and external stabilisation requirements; in the *United Kingdom,* monetary targets have been explicitly related to the Government's fiscal stance and other intermediate objectives. In view of external financing constraints, most of these countries had, at least temporarily, to give preference to control of domestic credit rather than the domestically held money stock.

Tables 1 and 3 reveal a wide spectrum of monetary and credit aggregates for which the monetary authorities have set projected values for twelve-month periods in recent years. The observed differences among countries result essentially from specific socio-economic conditions and national institutional arrangements under which the most appropriate intermediate control variables had to be selected. In implementing these quantity targets, major central banks have not adhered rigidly to medium-term "rules" for monetary growth. The authorities aim rather at greater long-run "steadiness" in monetary management without abandoning moderate discretionary use of policy instruments. The actual degree of operational flexibility has varied among countries and with changing economic conditions. European central banks, in particular, have emphasised the experimental nature of the new policy procedures. Periodic target-fixing thus usually proceeds from judgement as to monetary trends observed during the base or reference period, seeks to accommodate desired or projected rates of output growth together with tolerable inflation, and may allow for anticipated changes in income velocity. There can be little doubt, however, that initial targets announced in *Germany* (8 per cent for 1975), *Canada* (10-15 per cent for 1975-1976), the *United Kingdom* (12 per cent for fiscal 1976-1977), and *France* ($12\frac{1}{2}$ per cent for 1977), appeared, at least ex post, to be tight in view of the overall economic situation. The authorities aimed at moderating price and exchange rate expectations while avoiding the risk of a contractionary "credit crunch". Moreover, official credit ceilings adopted in *Italy* and the *United Kingdom* gave priority to a significant turnaround in external positions over a one to three year horizon.

Monetary authorities have not felt committed to realise their intermediate monetary objectives precisely—or observe them strictly as constraints—over twelve-month projection periods, nor have the authorities aimed at straight-line achievement of mid-point "nominal" monthly or quarterly target trajectories, consistent with annual projections, during a given year (Table 3). The short-run behaviour of monetary aggregates, which is statistically rather volatile, can, as a rule, not be predicted with precision. Smooth achievement of short-run trajectories may therefore necessitate large, erratic variations in market interest rates without improving the stability of the real economy or calming the public's price and exchange rate expectations. Abstaining from direct quantitative control of the reserve money stock or broader monetary aggregates in the very short-run, central banks generally implement their policies through flexible handling of traditional monetary instruments. In the *United States, Germany, Canada* and *Switzerland,* the authorities essentially rely on controlling money market conditions, with short-term interest rates transmitting the authorities' intentions—through bank portfolio behaviour and the public's money and bank credit demands—to the money stock. Complementary quantitative measures are used in *Japan*

Table 3. PROJECTED AND ACTUAL RATES OF MONETARY GROWTH

Country	Aggregate	Period	Target[a]		Outcome[a]	
			M1	M2	M1	M2
United States	M1/M2[b]	March 1975 - March 1976	5-7½	8½-10½	5.0	9.6
		1975 Q.2 - 1976 Q.2	5-7½	8½-10½	5.2	9.5
		1975 Q.3 - 1976 Q.3	5-7½	7½-10½	4.6	9.3
		1975 Q.4 - 1976 Q.4	4½-7½	7½-10½	5.7	10.9
		1976 Q.1 - 1977 Q.1	4½-7	7½-10	6.3	10.9
		1976 Q.2 - 1977 Q.2	4½-7	7½-9½	6.6	10.7
		1976 Q.3 - 1977 Q.3	4½-6½	7½-10	7.8	11.0
		1976 Q.4 - 1977 Q.4	4½-6½	7-10	7.8	9.8
		1977 Q.1 - 1978 Q.1	4½-6½	7-9½	7.7	8.7
		1977 Q.2 - 1978 Q.2	4½-6½	7-9½	8.2	8.4
		1977 Q.3 - 1978 Q.3	4-6½	6½-9	8.0	8.2
		1977 Q.4 - 1978 Q.4	4-6½	6½-9	7.2	8.6
		1978 Q.1 - 1979 Q.1	4-6½	6½-9	4.8	7.1
		1978 Q.2 - 1979 Q.2	4-6½	6½-9	..	..
Japan	M2[c]	1977 Q.3 - 1978 Q.3	11-12		12.0	
		1977 Q.4 - 1978 Q.4	12		12.6	
		1978 Q.1 - 1979 Q.1	12		12.2	
Germany	Central bank money	end-1974 - end-1975	8		10.0	
		Average 1975 - 1976	8		9.2	
		Average 1976 - 1977	8		9.0	
		Average 1977 - 1978	8		11.5	
		1978 Q.4 - 1979 Q.4	6-9			
France	M2	Dec. 1976 - Dec. 1977	12½		13.9	
		Dec. 1977 - Dec. 1978	12		12.3	
		Dec. 1978 - Dec. 1979	11			

Country	Aggregate	Period	M3 £	DCE	M3£	DCE
United Kingdom	Sterling M3 DCE	Fiscal year ending April 1977	9-13[d]	£9.0bn	7.8	4.6
		Fiscal year ending April 1978	9-13	£7.7bn	14.9	3.9
		Fiscal year ending April 1979	8-12	£6.0bn	11.4	6.7
Italy	Total domestic credit	March 1974 - March 1975	Lit. 21,800bn		19,600	
		March 1975 - March 1976	Lit. 24,700bn		35,280	
		Dec. 1975 - Dec. 1976	Lit. 29,500bn		33,280	
		Dec. 1976 - Dec. 1977	Lit. 32,000bn[e]		35,652	
		March 1977 - March 1978	Lit. 30,000bn		39,265	
		Dec. 1977 - Dec. 1978	Lit. 46,000bn		50,060	
		Dec. 1978 - Dec. 1979	Lit. 53,000bn			
Canada	M1	1975 Q.2 - 1976 Q.2	10-15		12.0[f]	
		Feb./Apr. 1976 - 1977 Q.2	8-12		7.0	
		1977 Q.2 - 1978 Q.2	7-11		9.5	
		1978 Q.2 - 1979 Q.2	6-10		..	

a) Absolute or percentage increase.
b) M3 targets, which have little operational meaning, are not shown.
c) Forecast.
d) Revised from 12 per cent to be consistent with DCE target.
e) Revised from Lit. 36 600 bn.
f) 1975 Q.2 - Feb./Apr. 1976 (excluding effects of postal strike).
Source: OECD Secretariat and national publications.

("window guidance" of bank lending), *France* (ceilings on bank lending and restraint of treasury bank borrowing), and the *United Kingdom* (public debt management and "corset" control of eligible interest-bearing bank liabilities). In *Italy,* as external disturbances and large scale monetisation of government debt reduced the efficiency of the "monetary base" as a control variable in the 1970s, the authorities have had to resort to a variety of quantitative restrictions (selective bank credit controls, bond investment ratios for commercial banks, limits on treasury borrowing from the central bank).

Short-run flexibility in operating strategy has not meant, however, that monetary targets have been regarded merely as non-committal projections or optional constraints with little effective influence on the direction of policy thrust. Indeed, monetary authorities have been reluctant to revise established objectives, even when the underlying economic situation might have justified such moves; the authorities have preferred to accept significant "over-shooting" or "under-shooting" over twelve-month periods, in the belief that such behaviour better preserved their credibility in the eyes of the public (Table 3). The authorities have, moreover, felt on many occasions that significant departures of monetary aggregates from projected trajectories over, perhaps, one to two quarters could be regarded as reliable predictors of undesired price or demand pressures. In such circumstances, the authorities have initiated corrective changes in money market conditions influenced by both monetary and basic economic considerations. Policy-controlled money market rates, the handling of direct policy instruments, and, to some extent, exchange rates, have thus shown some tendency to become "endogenised", i.e. inversely linked to the behaviour of monetary aggregates. This sort of policy response would ideally serve to keep monetary management on a stabilising course, avoiding excessively long recognition and policy action lags, reducing exposure of monetary authorities to ephemeral pressures, and exerting a credible influence on expectations in the home economy and international financial markets.

After several years of experience, these "new policy approaches" appear to have come somewhat under strain. Changing policy priorities have raised the public's sensitivity to possible output costs resulting from cautious target-constrained monetary management, and the technical difficulties of day-to-day policy implementation are more generally appreciated. More specifically, reconciliation of restrictive monetary targeting with employment-supporting budgetary policies and smooth financing of cyclically-inflated budget deficits has become an important issue. Similarly, the pursuit of domestically oriented monetary aggregate objectives and management of the exchange rate proved to be more difficult to reconcile than initially expected. The view has been expressed that the modest economic performance of many OECD Member countries in recent years owes much to governments' reluctance—or lack of perceived room for manœuvre—to pursue more ambitious growth and employment targets through discretionary adjustments of the main policy levers. On the other hand, some of those who view abnormal investor uncertainty as the salient feature of the past four years argue that hesitant monetary stabilisation efforts in many countries have prolonged the high inflation and unemployment problems. These unresolved issues point to a necessity to analyse more explicity the instrumental problems inherent in the present situation and to identify more clearly the present and future role of target-oriented monetary management.

In order to promote a discussion of these issues, the present paper provides a critical review of recent monetary policy experience in the seven larger OECD economies as well as some selected smaller countries which have shown clearly identifiable but differing attitudes as to the usefulness of target-oriented monetary management (*Belgium, Denmark, Switzerland*). Part I lays out—taking a rather simplifying approach—policy-relevant tenets and propositions in contemporary monetary analysis in an attempt to help clarify the conceptual background of the "new approaches" in monetary policy. Quantitative foundations and methods for implementing intermediate monetary objectives are discussed on a cross-country basis. Part II describes in some detail, for each of the seven largest OECD countries, the transition to monetary aggregate policies, its proximate motivation, target implementation, and the performance of target-constrained monetary management, mainly covering the period from 1974 to the end of 1978. Part III summarises, in a highly tentative manner, the evidence to date on monetary and general economic performance in countries practising monetary targeting, and advances cost and benefit criteria for assessing the adequacy of target-oriented monetary policies in the light of macroeconomic stabilisation objectives. Two Annexes supplement Part II: Annex I contains comprehensive analytical country charts for the seven largest economies; Annex II reviews the experience of smaller open economies. A selected bibliography (Annex III) contains the most important sources used and may serve as a reference for studying in greater detail some of the problems dealt with in the present study.

I
CONCEPTUAL AND QUANTITATIVE ASPECTS OF MONETARY TARGETING

This Part examines the rationale for target-oriented monetary policies and then describes some of the empirically important issues that have been spotlighted by academic discussion or by central bank experiences with targeting. Section A presents the contributions to the debate that have been made by diverse groups or "schools" of economists; section B then summarizes the apparent influence of those schools on official practices. In section C, the question is whether monetary "rules" should be imposed on monetary authorities on either political or technical grounds. Finally, section D discusses the criteria by which the authorities might choose among the available aggregates in focusing on a single or a dominant target.

A. THE RATIONALE FOR TARGET-ORIENTED MONETARY MANAGEMENT

The flexible approach to monetary targeting adopted by the monetary authorities in larger OECD countries has been based on pragmatic rather than dogmatic considerations. It reflects the development of a mainstream of economic thought that combines elements from earlier neo-Keynesian, monetarist and related analytical model structures. Public opinion, however, still tends to associate monetary targeting with monetarism. This lends a controversial flavour to the current policy discussion which is hardly warranted. Central banks and treasuries understandably have been reluctant to have their policy intentions, strategies and tactics linked with hard-core or popularised monetarist propositions. In the early stages of the monetarist controversy during the 1950s and into the 1960s, the case for monetary aggregates control did seem to be predicated on a set of extreme assumptions concerning the statistical exogeneity of the money stock, direct linkages from money to prices and real output, and stability of the velocity of money. The cruder versions of these propositions were invalidated by empirical evidence in many countries before publicly announced targets were considered seriously or put into operation. The current mainstream in monetary analysis does, at best, incorporate a milder form of early monetarism to the extent that the empirical reliability of monetary relationships—in particular the determination of demand for money through key macroeconomic variables such as wealth, income and interest rates—is broadly accepted. On the other hand, most adherents to modern monetarist strands of thought would now readily admit that the interaction of financial and real variables and the short-run monetary transmission process can be analysed in the broad structural model framework adopted by other academic schools.

Academic discussion has contributed to the analysis of the appropriate conduct of monetary policy through the development—within a rather common general framework—of several classes of specific macroeconomic models in which the role of money and other financial variables is explicitly identified. The following paragraphs employ a fairly standard categorization of these approaches into "schools", although overlapping among them has become substantial. Most notably, the popular use of the term "monetarism" to characterize the argument that the money stock plays a strong and predictable role in macroeconomics is clearly inappropriate and avoided here. Nonetheless, there is still an identifiable school of monetarists who—often by taking extreme but persuasive positions—have clearly contributed substantially to the debate over monetary targeting. Other important groups include those economists who have developed the monetary aspects of Keynesian models of aggregate demand, in the following referred to as neo-Keynesians, and several groups who might broadly be classified as portfolio theorists. The present description of these groups concentrates on the conflicting positions taken on the macroeconomic role of money, the need or scope for monetary stabilisation policies, and the choice of optimal financial control variables. Some tentative suggestions are advanced in order to identify the proximate analytical propositions built into current monetary management policies.

Neo-Keynesian and portfolio-balance modelling

During the first postwar decade and into the early 1960s, many monetary economists—generally regarded as followers of Keynes—took the position that financial variables should have little impact on the real economy due to the presumed insensitivity of real expenditures to the cost of funds. That proposition appears much less valid today, and the modern neo-Keynesian school accords an important role to financial variables in general and to money in particular. The term "neo-Keynesian model", which appears frequently in this discussion, refers to a class of models that provide a disaggregated explanation of aggregate demand and in which financial variables influence total expenditure through a variety of channels. These channels typically include the cost of capital, measures of financial wealth, credit rationing and possibly administrative controls. In contrast to simple non-monetary "Keynesian" structures, large-scale econometric models built in the neo-Keynesian tradition generally reveal significant expenditure multipliers for monetary policy variables. In contrast to most reduced-form "monetarist" "St-Louis"-type models, they generally suggest lasting effects also for pure fiscal policy action. The effects of both types of policy on real output tend to build to a peak over a two-to three-year period and then taper off as inflationary forces or financial crowding-out phenomena cumulate. The generality of these results has made neo-Keynesian econometric models a valuable policy simulation tool for the monetary authorities of many larger economies.

Several post-war approaches to macroeconomic theory have been based on the premise that a broad range of financial assets is relevant to expenditure determination, rather than a narrow subset such as the aggregates classified as money. Major contributions include those of the "Yale School" and Gurley and Shaw in the *United States*, the "Radcliffe Report" and the "new Cambridge School" in the *United Kingdom*. The existence of a wide spectrum of non-bank financial intermediaries and large stocks of government debt in most of the larger economies has given some credence to these views, according to which variations in the money stock are seen to be mirrored by offsetting movements in other financial assets that serve as close substitutes. On this view, monetary policy should be designed so as to avoid destabilising the financial system, generally by stabilising movements in interest rates and stock market yields rather than by control of monetary growth rates. The empirical relevance of these portfolio approaches has, however, been questioned by an extensive econometric literature on demand functions for specific monetary assets and on the money supply process. The bulk of the available macroeconomic research, as well as microeconomic analysis of bank structure and behaviour, suggests that—in most countries and under most conditions—the demand for money is sufficiently stable to warrant focusing financial control on a relatively narrow subset of monetary assets rather than total credit; and neo-Keynesian econometric models—a preferred policy-making tool in major countries—nearly always embody this stronger monetary hypothesis defended by mainstream analysis. However, not too much should be made of the contrast between these approaches; a complete "portfolio balance" model of financial flows like that recently published by the U.K. Treasury[1] necessarily has within it an implied demand for money function as well as the explicit relationships determining purchases of various forms of public sector debt.

Neo-classical "rationalism"

More recent and extremely rigorous arguments against flexible monetary management are embodied in specific versions of "neo-classical" models of price or exchange rate determination. These conjectures rest on the notion that policy-induced shifts in aggregate demand can affect real output only through *unexpected* changes in the price level, as the latter raise or depress the level of "real" interest rates or "real" wages. A "rationally" reacting public is hypothesised to translate accelerations or decelerations in monetary growth immediately into price effects and adjust nominal wage and interest claims in an equiproportionate manner, with "money illusion" no longer existing. Discretionary shifts in monetary policy are accordingly expected to be frustrated and could not affect real output and employment ("natural rate" hypothesis). Similarly, changes in monetary policy are held to feed instantaneously into nominal exchange rate adjustments, which respond to policy-induced changes in anticipated international inflation rate differentials. This process would erode the effectiveness of active stabilisation policies in "open" economies.

An implication of this extreme form of "rational expectations" model is that monetary policy would best focus on stable monetary growth, accommodating real growth at the potential output rate plus an allowance for fully anticipated inflation. On a theoretical level, the predictions made from neo-classical rational expectations mechanisms rest rather heavily on the assumption of perfect foresight and information, absence of fixed-term contracts, complete international integration, and equilibrium adjustment behaviour of the private sector of the economy. Basic behavioural features depicted in these models could bear some resemblance to abnormal price and exchange market reactions observed since the mid-1970s; but the hypothesis has so far been subjected to few rigorous empirical tests.

Monetarism

Modern monetarism is based on the belief that changes in nominal income are determined ultimately by variations in the growth rate of the stock of money, somehow defined. In a closed economic system (either a large country or a group of interdependent economies) policy-generated changes in the money

---

1. "A Financial Sector for the Treasury Model", Treasury Working Paper No. 8, December 1978.

supply are held to produce a macroeconomic disequilibrium in the form of an excess supply of money balances. Being determined largely by longer-term average or expected income and yields on alternative assets (both real and financial) and the level of actual income, the demand for money by private wealth holders will tend to rise over time to restore assets holders' portfolio balance. In combination with a view that real output is determined ultimately by aggregate supply conditions, this proposition implies that inflation, in the long-run, is almost purely a function of monetary growth. In this general form, monetarism allows for changes in the velocity of money during the business cycle, which, in principle, leaves room for discretionary monetary action. At the technical level, the "monetarist" argument against flexible monetary policy is based instead on the belief that the transmission process is not sufficiently well understood nor sufficiently quick to enable the authorities to take appropriate stabilizing measures.

Global monetarism

Concentrating on the position of dependent open economies under fixed exchange rates, a recent academic school known as "global" monetarism has questioned the efficiency of monetary management on balance of payments grounds. Independent monetary action taken in individual countries is claimed—in the extreme case—to be offset completely through capital and reserve movements which determine the home country's money market rates and money stock. On this view, only domestic credit expansion may be controllable in the individual country and the authorities could use this policy lever for influencing reserve movements and the balance of payments. Monetary policy could, in dependent economies, pursue domestic price and employment goals only within the scope created through capital controls and other obstacles to international integration, or through exchange rate flexibility. The policy prescription of "global monetarism" is for larger economies to control jointly the aggregate "world money stock" in order to keep world commodity prices and output at desired levels. The mechanism emphasised in the "world money stock" hypothesis can be empirically important in countries conducting monetary policies under external constraints. But the underlying assumptions are extreme. It has therefore been suggested by rival schools of thought that the equilibrating characteristics elaborated by this particular strand of monetarism should be incorporated and scaled down to appropriate levels of relevance in a more general model of the balance of payments adjustment process.

B. RECENT TENDENCIES IN OFFICIAL THINKING

As a broad synthesis is emerging from present neo-Keynesian and monetarist theoretical positions, it is becoming widely accepted, by both academic and government economists in most larger countries, that a certain class of monetary assets—which may, however, be difficult to define precisely—plays an important role in the determination of output, prices and external developments. This has prepared the ground for assigning a key indicator or yardstick function to the money stock in short-term monetary management. Exceptions to this conclusion generally reflect conditions specific to certain countries. The lasting difficulty of successfully measuring the demand for money in *Italy*, combined with continuous concerns about exchange rate and balance-of-payments control, makes that country a somewhat exceptional case. The Bank of Italy accordingly charts its policies with the aid of a flow-of-funds econometric model in which the growth and allocation of credit throughout the economy is more important than money as usually defined. Monetary thinking in *Belgium,* which may be shared broadly by a number of smaller countries, embraces a position of sophisticated skepticism that also incorporates elements close to the modern portfolio-balance approach. The Belgian authorities favour the control of total credit and liquidity and aim at selectivity and flexibility in day-to-day central bank intervention in the financial sector. *Danish* monetary policy, which has been dominated by external considerations, appears to reflect a "Mundell" solution of the policy assignment problem under fixed exchange rates; that approach suggests the use of monetary policy, at least in the short run, for controlling capital flows and the exchange rate as long as domestic unemployment is associated with a weak current account position.

Current central banking practices thus incorporate both a widespread application of flexible targeting (in larger countries) and various portfolio-balance approaches to monetary management (in several smaller economies). In the former, the authorities recognise the traditional role of the central bank as lender of last resort and believe in the relevance of short-run variations in financial yields for influencing monetary (supply or demand) relationships and the real sector of the economy in a predictable manner. These pragmatic attitudes (which recognise the possible harmful effects of the interest rate fluctuations) weaken the case for strict adherence to fixed targets for monetary growth. In the portfolio approach, scepticism about the importance of a single subset of financial assets defined as money has favoured a wider focus in which interest rates and/or comprehensive quantitative control of domestic credit flows and international capital movements play a major role. The influence of something closer to monetarist thought may be seen most clearly in *Switzerland,* where policies in recent years have, in a pragmatic and experimental manner, been based on a strong view of the importance of steady and moderate rates of monetary growth, at least in a medium to long-term sense. And in the *United States,* the wide spectrum of stated views facilitated by the federally structured central banking system has left room for a significant core of monetarist thought.

In larger countries with recurrent balance of payments difficulties, the adoption of quantitative intermediate objectives has typically responded to both domestic and external stabilisation requirements. In these countries, certain aspects of "rational expectations" models and "global monetarism" seem to have gained a degree of political relevance. The clearest example has been the *United Kingdom,* where a build-up of destabilising expectations led the Chancellor of the Exchequer to announce publicly a target for M3 in mid-1976. A standby loan arrangement concluded with the International Monetary Fund (IMF) in December of that year, emphasized the control of a related aggregate, domestic credit expansion (DCE). Similarly, monetary policy in *Italy* from 1974 through 1978, in the context of borrowing arrangements, is based essentially on a monetary concept of short-run balance of payments control. This view, which might be considered to be a moderate form of "global" monetarism, recognizes explicitly the importance of international financial integration and places considerable emphasis on the firm control of domestic credit growth for correcting external disequilibria.

C. POLICY-MAKING UNDER UNCERTAINTY

Rules versus discretion

A number of theoretical approaches have suggested the wisdom of limiting the scope for discretionary government policies, and these proposals may have contributed to the recent popularity of monetary targeting. On the broadest philosophical level, the imposition of operating rules has appealed to those—in both academic and government capacities—who wish to limit the role of government and the degree of discretion required of the central bank. Those who hold this position tend to combine confidence in the self-stabilising properties of the economy with scepticism about the timing of policy actions and effects; such attitudes have typically characterised adherents to monetarist tenets. In the early stages of the development of monetarism, the imposition of appropriate monetary rules was thought to require constant rates of growth for the stock of a monetary aggregate, at least in the medium term. Today it is widely accepted that a monetarist framework is, in principle, fully consistent with the application of active monetary policies, in particular to offset the effects of "supply shocks" to the economy. Nevertheless, distrust in the political wisdom and technical capabilities of governments still induces many monetarist policy commentators to prefer rules to discretion in the concrete case.

On a more technical level, the case for the imposition of monetary rules has focused on the existence of "long and variable" policy lags. Emphasis is placed on lags between the implementation of policy actions and their effects. When monetary policies are implemented through such indirect instruments as open market operations or changes in official lending rates, the effects might build up for several quarters before they have their dominant impact on spending decisions. Delays in the recognition of circumstances appropriate to a shift in the direction of policy or in the implementation of decisions are also important. These lags would seem to require the authorities to be able to forecast economic events reasonably well if they are to avoid destabilising the economy through inappropriately timed policy actions.

"Optimal" Economic Control

Whether central banks possess the technical capabilities to implement appropriate and timely countercyclical policies is a question that has been subjected to substantial empirical testing, notably in a rapidly growing literature applying the theory of optimal control.[2] Although most of this research relies heavily on econometric structures reflecting conditions in the *United States* economy and a philosophy that remains broadly neo-Keynesian, the results achieved so far may be relevant for monetary policy in general. In brief, simulation exercises using econometric models that incorporate detailed and integrated financial blocks have generally suggested that discretionary monetary management can improve the performance of the economy. Strict adherence

---

2. "Control-theoretic" applications implicitly recognise a need for stabilisation policies and governments' potential ability and will to act, but otherwise reduce the problem of optimal control to a technical "engineering" issue void of normative presumptions. Within this framework, monetary authorities are represented by an "objective function" to be optimised. This is usually formulated in terms of deviations of exogenous monetary "control" variables (e.g. interest rates) and of endogenous "state" variables (e.g. income) from desired values. Deviations are to be kept at a minimum, observing "boundary conditions". The latter are represented by initial values and desired values of variables in the system usually given by a dynamic econometric model. To map out an optimal control path, the model is "inverted", i.e., the position of "control" variables is made dependent on desired values for "state" variables. Apart from clarifying basic technical issues in fully "deterministic" structures (which in reality are hardly ever given), the approach serves to set up efficient operating rules within "stochastic" models of the economy (i.e., conditions characterised by additive random disturbances in the monetary and real sector of the economy, or uncertainties surrounding parameters in financial and real sector block equations). "Constraints" can be imposed in the procedure representing policy-makers' preferences, including "constant" or "steady" monetary growth rate rules, or "penalisation" of "excessive" fluctuations in interest rates.

to a constant monetary growth rule is suggested as an optimal strategy only in the absence of exogenous shocks or in a particular but unusual combination of circumstances such as those existing immediately after the 1974 oil crisis. The models do confirm the importance of policy lags, but the results from competing models are by no means free of conflict. Thus, while there does not appear to be any technical justification for abstaining altogether from active monetary policies, the evidence may indicate the desirability of reduced levels of ambition in this regard.

Another empirical rationale for the shift in emphasis towards monetary aggregates is the growing awareness of the limited reliability of information about the likely impacts of movements in interest rates. In principle, and leaving aside constraints arising from central bank or government preferences, the choice between money stock control and interest rate control is a trivial exercise in neo-Keynesian macroeconomics. Under the strongest assumptions about the policy-maker's knowledge of the economy—essentially, assuming the absence of random disturbances—any desired growth rate for GNP could be achieved equally well by:

a) controlling growth in the money stock and allowing interest rates to vary endogenously, or
b) controlling interest rates at the appropriate level and allowing the money stock to vary endogenously.

In practice, the information derivable from observation or from econometric evidence provides only imperfect guidance as to the predictable consequences of either type of policy. The superior strategy might be considered to be the one that minimizes the expected policy error (e.g., the lowest simulated departure of GNP from its desired values). Then if uncertainties in the projection of interest-sensitive expenditures dominate, the money stock would provide the better policy guide; if errors result mainly from instabilities in monetary relationships, control of interest rates would be preferred. The ideal policy would be to devise a control-theoretic strategy based on deviations of both aggregates and interest rates from projected paths. But with the possible exception of the *United States,* available econometric models are not sufficiently reliable or detailed to generate viable multivariate control options.

This error-minimising criterion now is widely believed to favour aggregate over interest-rate strategies. For a variety of reasons, and abstracting from occasions of structural and institutional change that have produced "shifts" in demand for money, linkages from market interest rates to final expenditures have proved more difficult to measure than have the corresponding monetary relationships. First, the market valuation of the services from capital goods (implicit rental value) is only weakly approximated by current interest rates, and the response of capital expenditures to changes in implicit rentals—generally thought to be an important channel for monetary impulses—may not be very strong and rapid. In contrast, aggregate money/income relationships have been measured fairly reliably through demand for money functions. Second, as expectations about inflation have become more important and more volatile in recent years, real interest cost of any given level of interest rates has become increasingly difficult to assess, and the information value of market interest rates may, at times, have been virtually eroded. Moreover, the mere existence of a broad range of interest rates that do not regularly move in tandem seriously weakens the informational value of those rates as guides for the conduct of monetary policies. Certainly all of these problems exist for monetary aggregates as well; but the associated difficulties appeared to be less severe in most of the larger economies when monetary strategies had to be developed in response to abnormal circumstances in recent years.

One further important result from control-theoretic research has been the application of an error-minimising criterion for the choice of short-run operational policy strategies. In the absence of comprehensive administrative powers, especially in highly developed financial systems, a simplified criterion juxtaposing the money stock and a key longer-term market interest rate may not suffice to enable the authorities to make confident decisions on appropriate operating procedures. The instruments available to central banks in larger countries including the *United States, Germany,* or *Canada* (open market operations, compulsory reserve ratios, official lending rates) enable the authorities to maintain more direct control over money market conditions than over intermediate financial variables such as monetary aggregates or bond rates. It may therefore be appropriate for these central banks to regard either bank reserves or a key short-term interest rate as the primary policy lever. The growth rate of the money stock becomes an "intermediate instrument", whose behaviour in relation to what is appropriate for the desired path of final expenditure triggers corrective adjustments in the primary instrument variable, *viz.* money market conditions.

D. CRITERIA FOR CHOOSING AMONG AGGREGATES

In choosing the most appropriate monetary aggregates with which to chart monetary management, central banks have been forced to operate with little directly applicable guidance from academic discussion. Mainstream monetary analysis has always suggested that money, strictly defined, plays a unique role in determining the value of the total flow of transactions. A collection of assets that functions primarily as a "medium of exchange" should, in theory, be more relevant than an aggregate that serves also as a depository for savings or permanent accumulation of financial wealth. But the conventionally measured monetary aggregates correspond only approximately to such analytical constructs; even broad definitions could be dominated by transactions balances. Certainly the issue must be settled—if at all—by empirical pragmatism. To some extent, choices might be influenced by the authorities' view of the plausibility of the target aggregate in the context of overall national policies (see Part II). Quantifiable factors which have further influenced choices among narrow and broad definitions of money or credit include:

a) the stability and predictability of relations between credit market conditions and monetary aggregate behaviour, and between the latter and final expenditure; and

b) the availability of manageable instruments and administrative powers.

The remaining paragraphs of this Part examine these latter issues.

Controllability

The first quantitative criterion that an aggregate must meet if it is to serve as an efficient policy guide or intermediate operating target is that it be broadly controllable by the monetary authorities through available instruments. Practices in this field vary among the major central banks, for reasons that are probably more institutional and historical than economic. Notably in the *United States, Canada* and *Germany,* where administrative intervention in financial markets traditionally has been kept to a minimum, policies are implemented predominantly through money market operations with direct impacts on bank reserve positions and short-term interest rates. These actions do not translate directly into changes in either broad or narrow stocks of money; control hinges on the authorities having sufficient time to assess and offset, if necessary, the consequent portfolio shifts by the public. When the central bank increases the supply of bank reserves through open market purchases, it expects to reduce temporarily money market interest rates. The demand for all types of bank deposits will thereby rise, but the extent of the effect depends, *inter alia,* on whether yields paid on time and savings deposits respond quickly to changes in each type of bank deposit as a close substitute for securities. The evidence from econometric studies suggests that demands for narrow and broad definitions of money respond similarly to changes in interest rates. More generally, the controllability criterion appears to offer little substantive support for a choice between aggregates in these countries.

Central banks in *Japan, France, Italy* and *the United Kingdom,* among others, have made extensive use of credit ceilings, supplementary deposits and related controls. These techniques are more readily applicable to the control of total credit expansion by banks than to growth in sight deposits alone. They tend thereby to limit the effects on broader aggregates of portfolio substitutions by banks or the public, especially where their use is associated with a high degree of rigidity in deposit yields. The use of credit controls therefore provides some justification for preferring M2 or M3 as the dominant control variable in these countries.

Predictability of effects

The other major quantitative criterion that a monetary aggregate must fulfill is that its control lead to stable and predictable effects on the economy. This criterion sometimes has been interpreted erroneously as implying stability of the income velocity of money (measured as the ratio of GNP or GDP to the stock of money). Certainly if velocity were either constant or dominated by a simple trend, changes in nominal income could be linked directly to changes in money stock; this would render the justification of a monetary target to the public comparatively easy, if not trivial. Unfortunately, velocity observations provide little comfort in this context. Income growth rates simply cannot be predicted reliably from velocity trends alone. In particular, velocity in most countries displays a significant cyclical component that appears to be related to variation in interest rates. If the authorities were to follow a simple operating rule of stabilising monetary growth at a medium-term rate, interest rates would tend to move countercyclically, rising in business upswings and falling during recessions. But these movements, being entirely endogenous or passive, would not in general be sufficient to prevent cyclical instability of the economy and would certainly be a misleading indicator of monetary thrust. Equally misleading would be the familiar procedure of measuring monetary ease or tightness from short-run changes in the gap between growth rates for nominal GNP and for the stock of money.

Table 4 presents some basic statistical comparisons of velocity trends for two or three aggregates in each of the larger economies. The first column indicates trend values for the 1965-1977 period. Except for M2 in the *United States,* all of the aggregates show some significant trend, usually positive for M1 (except in *Italy* and *Japan*) and invariably negative for the broader definitions. But only in the case of M1 in the *United States* does the trend explain as much as 90 per cent of the quarterly variation in velocity during the period examined. In most cases between one fourth and one half of the quarterly variation remains to be explained. The magnitude of the errors that would result from reliance on a simple trend relationship for velocity for financial projections is suggested by the third column, which lists standard errors as percentages of the mean values. For most countries (the *United Kingdom* excepted), the broader aggregates involve somewhat smaller errors than M1. However, all of the measured errors are sufficiently large to raise doubts about the wisdom of relying on these simple statistical relationships for extrapolating monetary developments. In every case examined here, the residuals in the trend equations are extremely autocorrelated (as indicated by the Durbin-Watson statistics in the final column). This indicates "mis-specification", i.e. determination of velocity through other factors beyond a time trend, in particular cyclical and interest rate effects.

Table 4. INCOME VELOCITY IN MAJOR OECD COUNTRIES, 1965-1977

		Trend (annualised, per cent)	R^2	Standard Error (per cent)	Durbin-Watson
United States	M1	2.65	.95	2.30	.12
	M2	0.07[a]	.03	1.43	.36
Japan	M1	−1.53	.53	5.70	.14
	M2	−1.31	.62	4.02	.16
Germany	M1	0.37	.09	4.64	.12
	M2	−1.11	.54	4.06	.15
	M3[b]	−1.32	.69	2.42	.33
France	M1	2.81	.84	4.65	.48
	M2	−1.84	.78	3.66	.61
United Kingdom	M1	2.77	.74	6.31	.81
	M3	−0.62	.10	7.36	.19
Italy	M1	−3.40	.65	9.97	.50
	M2	−2.40	.76	5.23	.90
Canada	M1	2.05	.88	2.97	.46
	M2	−1.63	.86	2.61	.35

Note: Calculations are based on quarterly nominal GNP/money stock data (V_i) for the period 1965 Q.1 - 1977 Q.4. The trend equation takes the form of $\log V_i = a_0 + a_1 t$.
a) t-statistic less than 2.0.
b) 1969-1977.
Source: OECD Secretariat.

A more revealing view of the money-income relationship can be gleaned from demand functions for the various money aggregates. Analysis of the demand for money functions is now applied by virtually all major central banks in countries that have adopted monetary targets. A recent study prepared for the OECD Secretariat presents estimates and stability tests for a set of demand functions for major OECD economies, the results of which are summarised in Table 5.[3] A specific question that has been posed in this study is whether the estimated functions have been stable over the recent period of high inflation, floating exchange rates and general economic disturbances. The case of M1 in the *United States* may serve as an example for collecting the relevant information from the summary evidence presented in Table 5. First, the direct test for instability of the demand function suggests that a break in the function probably occurred around the end of 1975 (the F-statistic being

---

3. J.M. Boughton "The demand for Money in Major OECD Countries", OECD Economic Outlook, Occasional Studies, January 1979.

above the critical level). Strongly supporting that impression is the information that a version of the equation estimated for a "truncated" sample ending in 1973 predicts badly for the 1974-1977 period. The full-sample equation predicts well, but the equation coefficients do not appear to be reliable. This general conclusion of instability of the demand for M1 in the United States has been corroborated by other recent econometric studies.

The broader aggregate (M2) appears to be more reliably estimated and possibly more stable than M1 in the *United States*; some instability may be present in both functions. Demand for broader aggregates may also be superior in *Canada, France* and *Japan*, though in each of those cases the functions estimated for M1 also work reasonably well. In *Germany,* the information content for M2 appears to be low, but the M1 and M3 functions both work well with a slight edge apparently in favour of M1. For the *United Kingdom*, M1 is clearly superior to M3, the latter having undergone significant distortion in the 1970s in response to the transition to new financial control procedures ("Competition and Credit Control" 1971), the changing pattern of interest rates, and policy controls over interest-bearing deposits. In *Italy,* neither narrow nor broad aggregates could be chosen from this evidence as a reliable guide for monetary policy, since the demands for M1 and M2 do not conform to the standard function. But with the exception of Italy, at least one conventionally

Table 5. STABILITY PROPERTIES OF DEMAND FOR MONEY FUNCTIONS FOR MAJOR OECD COUNTRIES

		Equations satisfactory?[a]	Parameters Stable?[b]	"F-Test" for Instability[c]	Forecast Accuracy[d], using:	
					Full Sample Statistic	Truncated Sample Statistic
United States	M1	No	No	4.9	.23	.64
	M2	Yes	Yes	2.6	.21	.27
Japan	M1	Yes	Yes	1.2	.20	.27
	M2	Yes	Yes	0.4	.09	.10
Germany	M1	Yes	Yes	2.4	.27	.31
	M2	Yes	No	7.3	.44	.68
	M3	Yes	Yes	2.2	.29	.31
France	M1	Yes	Yes	6.3	.52	.56
	M2	No	No	4.3	.35	.40
United Kingdom	M1	Yes	Yes	0.7	.40	.41
	M3	No	Yes	0.9	.24	.46
Italy	M1	No	No	13.7	.58	.71
	M2	No	Yes	5.9	.42	.54
Canada	M1	Yes	Yes	1.2	.64	.66
	M2	Yes	Yes	1.3	.27	.49

a) The equations and the stability tests are described in detail in Boughton (1979). They have been labelled "satisfactory" in this table if the parameters are in the "expected" range and are generally statistically significant.
b) This column indicates whether the overall qualitative pattern of the equation is the same when the last four years (16 observations, 1974-1977) are dropped from the sample used for estimation.
c) The statistics in this column have been computed for a comparison between full-sample (generally 1960-1977, quarterly) and truncated-sample estimates (ending in 1973.IV). Values above approximately 2.3 suggest the possibility of instability.
d) These statistics, known as "Theil coefficients", take on values between zero and one. Values "close" to zero indicate relatively accurate forecasts.

defined monetary aggregate in each country examined could be said to provide useful information about the likely consequences of policy actions. It must be noted, however, that all of the functions estimated in this study depend significantly on interest rates and inflation as well as income. It would not be warranted to attempt to predict growth in income or prices simply from projections about the likely or desired growth of either M1 or M2.

II

EXPERIENCE WITH MONETARY TARGETING

This Part reviews in some detail recent experience with monetary aggregates control in the seven major OECD countries. Although the presentation is not strictly uniform, each of the following country sections addresses the following main topics:
 a) the selection and specification of intermediate monetary targets based on monetary aggregates,
 b) the instruments for implementing them,
 c) monetary and general economic performance following the transition to target-oriented monetary management, with particular attention to those economies where monetary targets have been published for a number of years (*United States, Germany, Italy, Canada*).

Two annexes supplement Part II. Annex I presents, on a broadly uniform basis, complementary graphical material. For each major country, monetary and fiscal policy indicators and general economic data representing macro-economic objectives have been juxtaposed. The resulting analytical sets of **Charts A and B should serve to facilitate an assessment of countries' performances.** Annex II discusses recent monetary policy experience in selected smaller countries in which the authorities have taken differing views as to the benefits of monetary targeting. The experience of the three countries considered—*Belgium, Denmark,* and *Switzerland*—cannot, of course, be generally representative. Nevertheless, the choice takes account of the variety of monetary policy options available to dependent open economies in the face of exchange rate or balance of payments pressures.

UNITED STATES

The philosophy of monetary management

Heightened public concern with monetary policy in the wake of the restrictive conditions which prevailed in 1974 and contributed to the ensuing recession led the U.S. Congress in April 1975 to request that the Federal Reserve report, on a quarterly basis, its monetary intentions for the year ahead. This action led, in the spring of 1975, to public release of twelve-month target ranges for key monetary aggregates. Preceding this Congressional request the Federal Reserve had been using longer-run monetary growth projections as an internal policy guide for several years. Starting in early 1966, policy directives issued by the Federal Open Market Committee (FOMC) instructed the System

Account Manager to influence money market conditions while observing quantity constraints—known as the "proviso clause"—with respect to desired rates of bank credit expansion. In the early 1970s, FOMC operating instructions generally emphasised bank credit and the money supply as short-run intermediate policy variables, with money market conditions assuming a less prominent role, while official views on the desired course of monetary aggregates were guided by longer-term financial and macroeconomic projections.

Federal Reserve policy decisions are the product of the FOMC's monthly evaluation of a broad range of information concerning the state of the U.S. economy. The degree to which observed and prospective behaviour of monetary aggregates influences policy varies. Medium-term projections on aggregates growth are expected to be consistent with a desired growth path of nominal GNP, so that, generally speaking, persistent deviation of actual aggregates growth from that projected is resisted. Such resistance comes more quickly when other data support the picture suggested by deviation of the aggregates. But when this is not the case, particularly if there is reason for suspecting a short-term shift in demand for money in relation to income, the FOMC may choose to respond much more gradually to observed aggregates growth outside the medium-term ranges. The evolution of Federal Reserve policy formation in the 1970s can be seen as a continuing effort to define operationally desired monetary growth, so as to avoid both unduly delayed counteraction and unnecessary reaction.

In the short term, the financial factors affecting the Federal Reserve's policy stance go beyond the current observed monetary growth rate, and include:

a) *Credit conditions.* For many years the FOMC has had a protective attitude toward what is generally referred to as "the sensitive state of the financial markets". Policy makers have sought to resist interest rate movements that were too abrupt or extreme and to avoid volatility in market interest rates. These concerns have led the authorities to be quite flexible at times in their willingness to tolerate deviations of monetary growth from the projected path, as long as the long-term aggregate stance was not expected to be affected. The concern with credit market conditions—in addition to the "lender of last resort" responsibility—is related in a broad manner to the state of the economy. More specifically, given the uncertainties surrounding the relationship between changes or volatility in short-term interest rates and overall economic activity, pre-occupation with credit market conditions has reflected concern about the interest-sensitivity of private expenditures and savings flows into thrift institutions and subsequent effects on the housing sector.

b) *The dollar position.* On occasion, notably during 1977 and 1978, Federal Reserve actions to ease money market conditions have been slowed, or actions to raise interest rates hastened, because of the weakness of the dollar in foreign exchange markets.

Generally speaking, the Federal Reserve's medium-term policy goal is to achieve moderate and declining growth in the monetary aggregates so as to choke off inflation gradually while accommodating non-inflationary growth. In some periods characterised by severe inflation shocks, the FOMC has shown itself willing to give priority to the anti-inflation goal, holding the line on monetary growth and accepting reduced real growth to avoid an inflation surge. In the short run, the Federal Reserve has sometimes tolerated monetary growth well outside previous projections when the consequences of monetary control on interest or exchange rates were likely to be extreme. More generally, when interest rate pressures are severe and the stability of short-run relationships between money and income is in doubt, the authorities are inclined to accommodate the change in the demand for money rather than risk missing their ultimate policy goals.

The implementation of policy

During the period of explicit monetary targeting, which began in 1975, the FOMC has implemented policy through a two-stage procedure (Chart 3). First, 12-month tolerance ranges for the quarterly growth of M1, M2 and M3 are set, or reaffirmed, along with an associated growth range for bank credit, based on the average level of each of these aggregates in the full quarter preceding each FOMC meeting.[1] These projections are based on broad staff estimates of monetary growth required to sustain forecast real income growth while containing the rate of inflation. Associated with these monetary and GNP growth estimates is a projected path for the interest rate on "Federal funds" (short-term, immediate-credit interbank loans). It is this rate which the Federal Reserve most directly controls through its operations in U.S. government securities in the money market. Secondly, two-month "tolerance ranges" are projected for growth of M1 and M2 which are thought to be consistent with the longer-term goals while taking into account current factors affecting the demand for money.[2] Depending on the current intensity of the FOMC's concern about credit market or foreign exchange market conditions and depending on the state of observed monetary growth relative to the short-run tolerance ranges, the System Account Manager is instructed to conduct open market operations so as to adjust the Federal funds rate within a range with varying degrees of flexibility over the forthcoming inter-meeting period.[3] If a situation of mutual inconsistency develops—i.e., observed monetary growth outside its tolerance range and the Federal funds rate at its tolerance limit—the FOMC must be consulted. The Federal funds rate may be moved from its stipulated range only if the Manager is specifically instructed to do so by the FOMC. In making his adjustment decisions regarding the Federal funds rate, the Manager is normally instructed to place approximately equal weight on each of the aggregates which are assigned a short-run tolerance range.

1. "M1-plus" was added to this set of aggregates in late 1978. Innovations legalized as of November 1, 1978, which in essence transformed many interest-earning deposits into cheque accounts, led to the introduction of this aggregate — which includes, apart from M1, commercial bank savings deposits, demand deposits at savings and loan institutions, NOW (negotiated order of withdrawal) accounts, and credit union share drafts. By early 1979, the Federal Reserve was considering a broad redefinition of M1. In addition, passage of the Full Employment and Balanced Growth Act of 1978 (the "Humphrey-Hawkins" Act) changed the practice for setting medium-term monetary growth objectives. The Act required the Federal Reserve to transmit to the Congress, early in each calendar year, a report reviewing recent economic developments and analysing prospects, and presenting the FOMC's objectives with respect to the growth of monetary and credit aggregates for the year. Thus, Federal Reserve practice will now be to establish ranges for aggregates growth early in each year to be applied to that year on a fourth quarter-to-fourth quarter basis. These ranges will be reassessed at mid-year and preliminary ranges for the next year then reported. The Federal Reserve reserves the right to take action in the interim if necessary.
2. From 1973 through early 1975, the FOMC used, in addition to M1 and M2 as short-term guides, a range on "reserves available to support private deposits" (RPD's), i.e. total reserves less those required against interbank and Federal government deposits. This measure proved to be highly variable in relation to total monetary growth and was abandoned as a short-term indicator.
3. The Account Manager is to act to move the Federal funds rate within its range when incoming data indicate that monetary growth is *i)* significantly departing from the *midpoints* of the two-month aggregates tolerance ranges, when the behaviour of the aggregates is the Committee's more important short-term priority ("aggregates" directives), or *ii)* approaching or moving beyond the *limits* of the two-months aggregates ranges, when credit conditions are uppermost among the Committee's short-run concerns ("money market conditions" directive).

Chart 3. FEDERAL RESERVE TARGET-SETTING AND IMPLEMENTATION

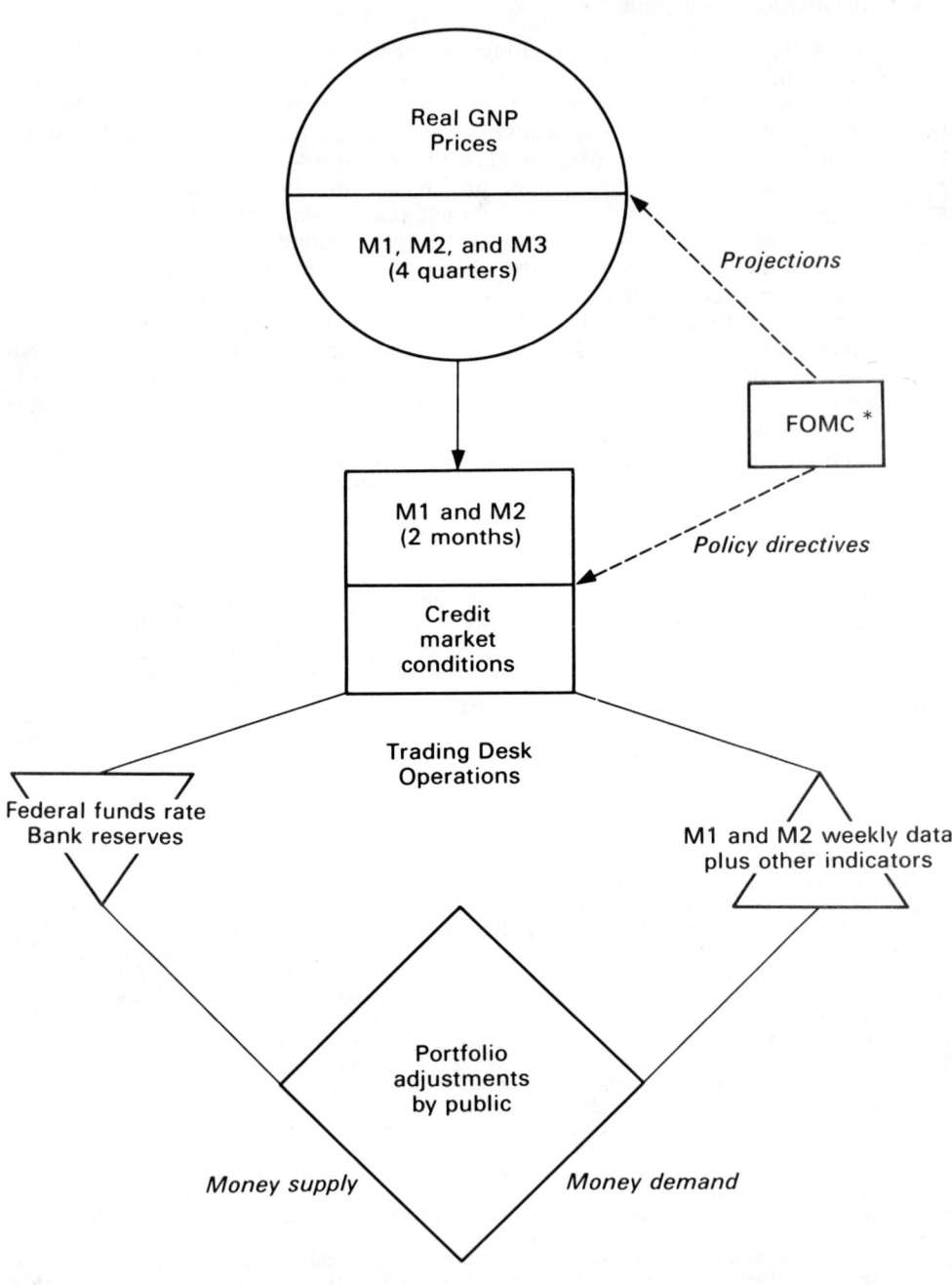

* Federal Open Market Committee.

Policy performance: mid-1975 through 1978

Any review of the record of monetary policy over the period of recovery that began in the United States in mid-1975 must recognise two salient facts of the economic environment over this period. First, the state of uncertainty with regard to future inflation and the associated persistence of high inflation expectations helped maintain a stubborn and substantial ongoing rate of price inflation; the price climate deteriorated in 1977-1978 due to dollar depreciation, food price surges, cost inflation associated with an increase in the minimum wage and in social security taxes, and cyclical wage pressures. Second, the rate of unemployment in the United States, though slowly declining, remained high through much of this period; it improved sharply only in late 1977/early 1978 (Chart A1). The state of the recovery frequently appeared tenuous to analysts until as late as the first quarter of 1978; in business sector decisions, the counterpart has been a persistent sluggishness in investment.

The policy implementation conflicts faced by the Federal Reserve over the past three years are evident from monetary data: although the tolerance ranges for growth of the monetary aggregates have been progressively lowered, the actual rates of growth of the aggregates have, on balance, edged progressively higher. This is most apparent in the case of M1 which grew at the lower limit of its range in the first year of the period under review, near the upper limit over the year from 1976 Q1, and well above the upper limits in 1977 and 1978 (Chart 4). A second set of important observations can be read from the policy records of the FOMC over this period: the specificity of credit conditions goals has increased; short-term aggregates ranges have become more flexible, in terms of both the width and the variability of tolerance ranges; and the willingness to adopt "money market conditions" directives has grown. At the same time, however, the Federal Reserve has shown itself more willing to adjust interest rate levels in anticipation of interest rate or, occasionally, exchange rate pressures that might otherwise be faced in quarters ahead.

It is clear from a review of Federal Reserve policy since 1970 that the Committee has been most willing to move firmly to contain monetary growth when the economy appeared to be advancing strongly on its own or when surging inflation has been a clear and present danger. When economic growth is strong, excessive monetary growth is considered a good short-to medium-term indicator of inflationary pressure in the economy and is firmly resisted. On the other hand, when economic growth has appeared to be weak, the information value of excessive monetary growth in relation to initial projections has been viewed with significantly greater suspicion by the FOMC, especially if inflation has been stable for some time. Thus, the picture of tentative recovery presented by data received through 1977 helps to explain the accommodative policy stance. Moreover, unexpectedly weak growth in M1 in relation to projections over 1975-1976 led the FOMC to lower the Federal funds rate rather dramatically, from $6\frac{1}{2}$ per cent (September 1975) to $4\frac{3}{4}$ per cent (April 1976). This action probably mitigated the "growth pause" of 1976, when real GNP growth decelerated to a $1\frac{1}{4}$ per cent annual rate in the fourth quarter from $8\frac{3}{4}$ per cent in the first quarter. However, the extent of the increase in M1 velocity that was occurring in 1976 may have been underestimated, setting the stage for sustained expansionary policies and later, excessive credit expansion.

The improvement in inflation which occurred over 1975-1977 may have contributed to the authorities' accommodative stance during that period. Over 1973-1974, U.S. consumer prices rose at an average annual rate in excess of 10 per cent. By early 1975 the rate had dropped to 6-$6\frac{1}{2}$ per cent, and it

Chart 4. MONETARY MANAGEMENT AND INTEREST RATE TRENDS: UNITED STATES

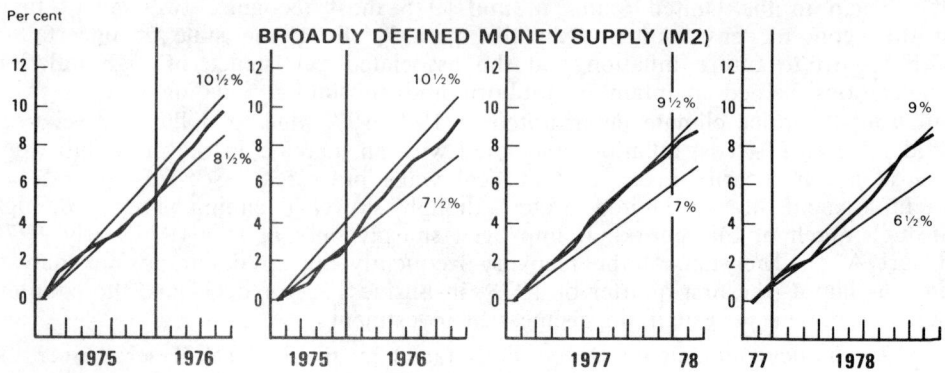

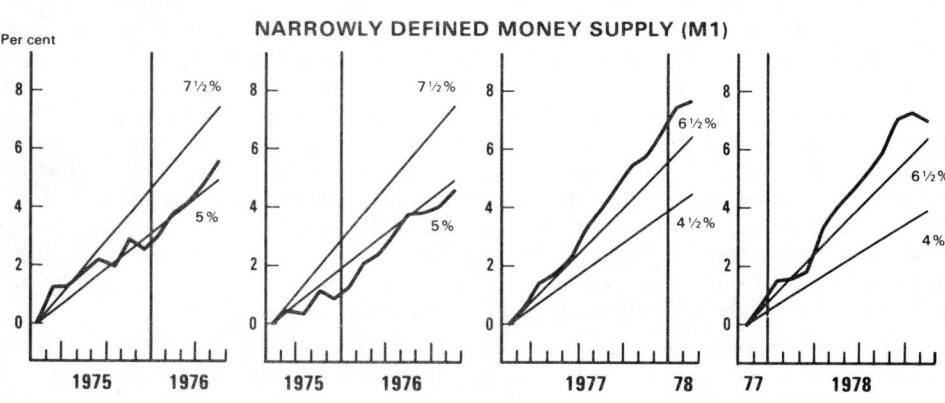

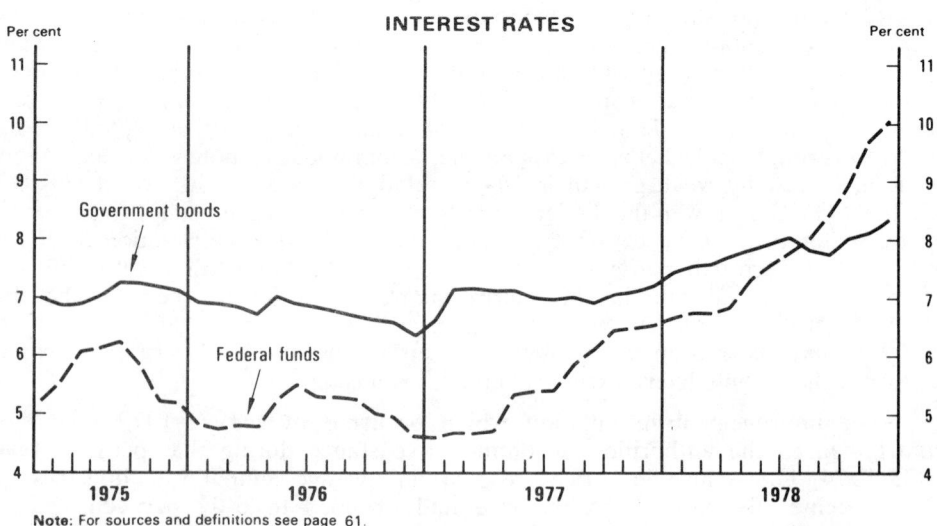

Note: For sources and definitions see page 61.

edged down further until mid-1977 (Chart A1). The stability of the inflation rate, albeit at a high level, moderated the urgency of action on this front, particularly given the high rate of unemployment that coincided with it.

Despite the fact that monetary growth, at least on the narrow definition, had been clearly above its upper limit during much of 1977 (Chart 4), the FOMC began to move more firmly to raise interest rates only in early 1978. This action was prompted less by excessive monetary growth (which in fact had moderated somewhat late in 1977) than by exchange rate weakness. By late 1977 the Committee had included instructions that the Federal funds rate be raised more readily within its range if the dollar were particularly weak. In early January 1978, the Federal funds rate was raised in a move specifically intended to support the dollar, an action that was to be repeated frequently during the remainder of the year. By the beginning of the second quarter, unemployment had declined to below 6 per cent, and inflation had re-emerged as a pressing policy problem. Though the FOMC raised interest rates rather sharply, the severity and persistence of the inflation surge may have been underestimated: interest rates did little more than follow the inflation rate. Consequently, little real restraint was felt on monetary growth, and by late summer of 1978 the aggregates had resumed the overshooting recorded in the spring. With the dollar's sharp decline in October, the Federal Reserve on 1st November moved to tighten credit conditions significantly, raising the discount rate a full percentage point to $9\frac{1}{2}$ per cent. The federal funds rate rose within a few weeks to around 10 per cent.

The important institutional changes legalized in late 1978 encouraged individuals to shift liquid assets from non-interest bearing demand deposits into savings accounts, and, at the same time, tended to reinforce trends distinguishing savings accounts and time deposits. These changes, along with the sharp upward shift in interest rates associated with the measures taken on 1st November, help account for the very slow growth of aggregates in the fourth quarter. Nevertheless, the year ended on note of substantial uncertainty with respect to the reliability of expected money-income relationships. As a result, and given evidence of ongoing economic strength and continued exchange rate sensitivity, the FOMC repeatedly overruled interest rate cuts as aggregates growth continued to be significantly below short-term ranges which had been widened on the down side.

With the benefit of hindsight, given the sharp increase in U.S. inflation that occurred after mid-1977, the clearest question that arises in a review of U.S. monetary policy over the 1975-1978 period is whether the authorities should have acted more firmly in resisting the above-range aggregates growth observed frequently during 1977. From March through August of that year, M1 increased at an average annual rate of some 10 per cent, well above the $6\frac{1}{2}$ per cent upper limit on the medium-term range. M2 growth over the period also averaged about 10 per cent, just above its upper limit. Meanwhile the Federal funds rate was slowly raised from the $4\frac{3}{4}$ per cent level that prevailed in early 1977 to reach 6 per cent at the end of August. Although the Federal Reserve's stance certainly was not the *cause* of the inflation upsurge, it does appear now that the overshooting of the aggregates was communicating information about the persistence of higher inflation, and that a more aggressive stance might have been justified. However, other contemporaneous data supported the gradualist policy actually followed. Thus the U.S. experience underlines the central question in aggregates-oriented monetary policy implementation: how quickly, in practice, should deviations from monetary objectives be counteracted?

JAPAN

Mirroring the experience of abnormally rapid inflation in 1973-1974, growing public concern about the inflationary consequences of "excess liquidity" creation and accelerating monetary expansion served to prepare the ground for a disinflationary monetary strategy, in which increasing attention has been paid to the growth of the money stock. Structural changes in the financial sector associated with liquid asset holding behaviour of the company sector and gradual shifts in the sectoral pattern of flow of funds have apparently undermined the reliability of bank credit expansion as an indicator of the thrust of monetary policy during the current decade. Precautionary holdings of liquid assets made the company sector less dependent on bank borrowing during periods of monetary tightness. Moreover, the accumulation of external assets through the banking sector and bank borrowing by the public sector began to claim significant shares among the broad money supply determinants in the early 1970s. Correlation analyses have accordingly pointed to a weakening link between changes in bank lending and economic activity in recent years. At the same time, changes in the broadly defined money stock (M2) have exhibited a significant statistical relationship with variations in output and domestic prices, although observed lag patterns have tended to be variable. During the period of exceptionally severe and prolonged monetary restraint from early 1973 to the spring of 1975, the Bank of Japan therefore gradually moved away from the traditional combination of the call money market rate and changes in city bank lending as intermediate policy-indicators, while increasing emphasis was placed on movements in the broadly defined money stock.

With strong inflationary pressures persisting, highest priority was given to restoring internal price stability during the tight monetary policy phase lasting into spring 1975. The increase in money supply was brought down sharply from 27.2 per cent at the end of 1972 to around 10 per cent at the end of 1974. As a consequence, the annual average percentage ratio between M2 and GNP ("Marshallian k")—a broad measure of domestic liquidity—declined markedly from a historically high level (80.8 per cent) to the trend value (76.4 per cent) during the period 1973 to 1974. The implied unprecedented tightening of monetary conditions was brought about through a strengthening of quantitative restrictions on bank lending and official selling operations in the private bill market combined with a restrictive lending policy by the central bank. The direct quantitative ceiling on bank lending was extended to include local banks and other financial institutions which had not been subjected to window guidance prior to 1973. The latter action seems to have eroded the role of the call money rate as a determinant of banks' opportunity cost with respect to ordinary earning asset holdings and thus their lending behaviour. Short-term money market rates, which exhibited wide fluctuations during the 1950s and the early 1960s in response to changing demand and supply conditions in the bank reserve market, appear, at least temporarily, to have almost lost their signalling and fund-reallocating function in the financial market. After switching to a moderately easy monetary policy stance in April 1975, the authorities nevertheless retained their cautious attitudes, maintaining firm quantitative control of bank lending. As a result, the rate of year-on-year monetary growth has been kept remarkably stable within a comparatively narrow margin ranging from 11 to 14 per cent during the period 1974 to 1978, while the official discount rate was brought down rapidly to a historically low level accompanied by a general downward adjustment of market interest rates including the most rigid deposit rates[4] (Chart B2).

Reflecting the encouraging experience in controlling the broad monetary aggregate since 1974 and the increasing evidence on the statistical properties of the new intermediate policy variable, the Bank of Japan decided to publish forecasts on broad money supply developments on a quarterly basis in July 1978. The announced range of year-on-year growth rates of M2 for 1978.Q3 and 1978. Q4 (11-12 and 12 per cent respectively) were regarded as broadly consistent with the ultimate policy objectives for output and prices. This included the assumption of a decelerating trend in price increases which was facilitated by the sharp appreciation of the exchange rate since early 1978. However, in commenting on its money supply forecasts, the Bank of Japan did not underline the mutual consistency between the projected path for the intermediate monetary aggregate and ultimate policy goals. The authorities, thus, appear to have deliberately refrained from a political commitment vis-à-vis the Diet. In retaining the freedom for flexible adjustments of projection values for monetary growth to changing short-run circumstances, the authorities can take account of behavioural shifts in asset holders' preferences and changes in financial practices without undue loss of credibility. This cautious attitude may well have been justified, given the possibility of significant changes in the desired level of private liquid asset holdings which could result from business firms' recent inclination to reduce their interest payment and debt burden and from the tendency towards greater diversification of financial portfolios observed in recent years. The actual rates of monetary growth in 1978.Q3 (12 per cent) and Q4 (12.6 per cent) were broadly in line with the forecast, mainly due to the accommodation of smooth sales of newly-issued government bonds in the financial market.

As long as the authorities are not obliged to engage in excessive support operations in the foreign exchange and bond markets, maintenance of monetary growth reasonably close to projection values is unlikely to pose insurmountable difficulties. A satisfactory monetary performance should be possible even on a quarterly basis since bank lending to the private sector is under very firm control. During the early 1970s, external disturbances and heavy intervention in the foreign exchange market seriously hampered effective monetary control, since the creation of "excess liquidity" could not be effectively prevented by employing traditional policy instruments. Exchange rate policy in Japan under the managed floating system appears to have been largely dominated by the principle of "leaning against the wind" without observing a target level of the exchange rate. However, heavy capital inflows in late 1977 and early 1978 created a potential source of monetary disturbance since the liquidity position of banks and the company sector was remarkably improved. The ratio of net money market liabilities of the banking sector to its total deposits declined sharply from 12.6 per cent in January 1978 to 9.3 per cent in April 1978, while the business sector showed an increasing preference for security holdings, entering the short-run bond trading market through repurchase agreements. Investment of firms' cash surpluses in securities together with their cautious borrowing behaviour contributed to the recent moderate rate of monetary expansion.

---

4. Given the maximum ceilings prescribed by the Temporary Interest Rates Adjustment Law (1947) on almost all market interest rates, deposit rates have been scarcely changed until the early 1970s. After the amendment of the law in April 1970, deposit rates were subjected to guidelines by the Bank of Japan, which allowed for greater flexibility of these rates.

On the other hand, massive flotation of government bonds within a relatively short period has tended to complicate the prudent management of monetary aggregates, given the present rigid issue terms and underwriting system.[5] A widening spread between yields offered to subscribers of new bonds and bond yields in the secondary market inhibited the issuance of large-scale public debt in the market, as long-term market rates on existing bonds tended to rise since April 1978. Against the background of a rapidly expanding short-run bond trading market with free interest rates, the earlier move towards liberalization of market interest rates in the money market was recently intensified by the Bank of Japan. This action was intended to ensure firm control over monetary aggregates and reinforce the effective transmission of monetary policy impulses through increased flexibility in interest rates.[6] The creation of bonds with a greater variety of initial maturities,[7] combined with the absorption of public debt through open market operations undertaken by the Trust Fund Bureau, might also help to facilitate the replacement of private deposit holdings by bond investments. However, further efforts may be needed to increase the private sector's willingness to hold government bonds in consolidating the control over monetary aggregates.

GERMANY

Transition to monetary targeting and policy concept

The adoption of a new quantity approach to monetary management by the Bundesbank suggested itself in the early 1970s when the reliability of banks' "free liquid reserves", the traditional key indicator of the thrust of monetary policy, was progressively eroded. Commercial banks apparently lowered the desired level of conventional secondary reserves, reflecting the expansion of the domestic interbank money market and a rapid integration of national and international money markets. By early 1973, the banks' holdings of "free liquid reserves" (including unutilised rediscount quotas at the Bundesbank) had been reduced to a historically low level while banks continued to increase their supply of credit, in sharp contrast to traditional portfolio behaviour. Following

---

5. The development in newly-issued central government bonds is presented in the table below:

Fiscal year	1975	1976	1977	1978	1979
Yen billion	5,280	7,200	9,985	10,990	15,270
Percentage ratio to nominal GNP	(3.4)	(4.2)	(5.2)	(5.2)	(6.6)

Source: Ministry of Finance.

6. See "Steps Towards Flexible Interest Rates in Japan", *Monthly Review of the Bank of Japan,* October 1977. The attempt to increase the flexibility of short-term interest rates found its expression in:
— more flexible changes in interest rates on resold private bills (June 1978)
— the introduction of seven day call loans with a free rate (October 1978)
— the introduction of one-month private bills with a free rate (December 1978)
— the introduction of certificates of deposits (May 1979).

7. In addition to the already existing bonds with maturities of ten and five years, three-year bonds for public offerings were issued in June 1978 in order to satisfy market needs for short-term assets and prevent an early increase in long rates. The diversification of government bonds was further pursued in 1979 through the flotation of two, four and seven year bonds.

the transition to a floating exchange rate system in March 1973, the authorities made considerable efforts to regain control over the creation of reserve money. At this stage, short-term foreign assets lost their earlier reserve quality[8] and domestic "free liquid reserves" effectively available to the banking system fell virtually to zero. In experimenting with a new operating strategy—which initially did not include an explicit intermediate target procedure—the authorities tolerated unusually tight monetary conditions, while the volatility of short-term interest rates assumed unprecedented proportions (Table 6). The resulting "trial and error" process reinforced the recognition that direct control of the stock of central bank money in the very short-run was hardly feasible without neglecting the central bank's "lender of last resort" function. In the process, a new operating procedure evolved under which short-term money market rates—controlled through changes in official lending rates and variations in bank reserves[9]—assumed the role of a control instrument, with the central bank money stock representing a key intermediate policy variable.

Table 6. GERMAN INTERBANK RATES 1973-1974
Per cent, per annum

		Call Money		One Month	
		Monthly Average	Range	Monthly Average	Range
1973	January	5.58	1¾-7	6.96	6½-7½
	February	2.18	⅛-7¼	6.50	5¾-7
	March	11.37	6¾-20	8.67	7-9½
	April	14.84	2-30	11.51	10-13
	May	7.40	½-14	11.69	10-13
	June	10.90	2-17½	12.43	10½-14
	July	15.78	2-30	13.29	12½-14
	August	10.63	6¾-40	12.14	10-15½
	September	9.76	½-18	13.30	12¾-14
	October	10.57	0-15½	13.18	12-14
	November	11.30	5¾-22	12.08	10½-13½
	December	11.89	8-13½	13.33	13-13¾
1974	January	10.40	3-13¼	11.68	10½-13
	February	9.13	6-12½	10.05	9-11⅛
	March	11.63	7-13	11.21	10 ⅝-11¾
	April	5.33	1-11¾	9.28	8-11⅜
	May	8.36	4¼-16	8.16	7¼-9½
	June	8.79	6.8-12	9.01	8.5-9.8
	July	9.40	8.8-11.5	9.23	8.5-9.8
	August	9.30	9.0-9.7	9.41	9.2-9.6
	September	9.22	9.0-9.6	9.41	9.2-9.6
	October	9.10	8.5-9.5	9.29	8.9-9.5
	November	7.38	4.7-8.7	8.21	7.5-9.2
	December	8.35	7.5-8.7	8.63	8.3-8.8

Source: Deutsche Bundesbank.

8. With official intervention against the U.S. dollar and most other currencies (except those of the mini-snake) being suspended, short-run foreign assets held by commercial banks could not be regarded as "potential" central bank money. Thus this component of bank liquidity was excluded from the definition of "free liquidity reserves" from February 1973.
9. The Bundesbank's neo-Keynesian macro-model accordingly "explains" the behaviour of the three-month interbank rate through the official Lombard rate and changes in banks' "free liquid reserves". Cf. "Further Development of the Econometric Model of the Deutsche Bundesbank", *Monthly Review of the Deutsche Bundesbank*, April 1978, pp. 22-31.

Experimenting at the money market level had passed through its early testing stages, when the Bundesbank—strongly supported by the government and the Council of Economic Experts—decided in late 1974 to publish an annual target for the growth of the central bank money stock during the twelve months ahead. The announced 8 per cent target rate was regarded as an intermediate monetary objective in the framework of a medium term strategy aiming at steadier monetary growth. Greatest importance was attached by the Bundesbank, the government and its advisors to conveying a credible announcement effect to the public, especially trade unions and employers (including public authorities). The monetary objective provided for monetary accommodation of moderate economic recovery while setting the state for a gradual winding-down of inflation. This public policy statement was prompted by the disappointing inflation performance of the preceding year, during which the unquantified announcement of non-accommodating monetary policy by the central bank had left both sides of industry largely unimpressed. The public announcement of an annual monetary target, which the Bundesbank has always regarded as "experimental", has since become a regular part of the policy "package deal" put forward in the government's Annual Economic Report at the beginning of each calendar year.

The intermediate target variable selected by the Bundesbank—the adjusted central bank money stock—includes currency in circulation and banks' minimum reserves on domestic bank liabilities at constant reserves ratios of January 1974.[10] This variable was considered to have clear advantages over other aggregates: its choice has been supported by stability tests; it appeals to the general public, as the measure puts the central bank's own contribution to monetary expansion conspicuously into focus; statistical information on most recent trends in the target variable are readily available; and the central bank money stock should be controllable through money market levers on the evidence of available research. The formal derivation of central bank money projections from government output and price objectives has been based on the following elements:

— anticipated potential output growth,
— a desired change in capacity utilisation,
— an "unavoidable" rise in prices (GNP deflator),
— an expected change in velocity allowing for both the cyclical position of the economy and past experience with monetary growth,
— the "carry over" in monetary growth resulting from the use of the annual average central bank money stock as a reference during the period 1975-1978.[11]

On the assumption that velocity and utilisation rate changes might broadly cancel out, the authorities would be able to "advertise" annual targets in a medium-term context, putting the emphasis on potential output growth and unavoidable inflation as the main arguments in deriving the monetary target. Contrary to the expected pro-cyclical rise in velocity, actual velocity exhibited an almost

---

10. The weights used for the calculation of adjusted central bank money stock are 16.6 per cent for sight deposits, 12.4 per cent for time deposits and 8.1 per cent for savings deposits, which corresponds to a weighting scheme of roughly 4:3:2. Thus the weighting scheme attributes an exceptionally high weight to currency in circulation relative to other components of the money stock.

11. The "carry over" in monetary growth represents the deviation of the level in December of the central bank money stock from its annual average. The same target growth rate based on the annual average level may imply different degrees of monetary tightness, according to different "carry over" rates during the period 1976-1978. Avoiding such ambiguous implications on monetary policy stance, the announced target growth rate for 1979 ranging from 6 to 9 per cent is derived from fourth quarter to fourth quarter changes.

anticyclical pattern (Table 7) in the current recovery phase, which, among others, may have reflected the abnormal liquidity preference of the company sector.[12]

Table 7. GERMANY:
CENTRAL BANK MONEY STOCK AND ITS DETERMINANTS
Projected (P) and Actual (A) Growth Rates in per cent

	1975 P	1975 A	1976 P	1976 A	1977 P	1977 A	1978 P	1978 A
Central bank money stock[a]	7¼[b]	7.8	8	9.2	8	9.0	8	11½
Nominal GNP	8½	4.7	9	9.2	9	6.3	7	7.4
Velocity of circulation	1¼	−2.9	1	—	1	−2.5	−1	−4
Potential output	2		2		3		3	
Real GNP growth	2	−2.0	4½	5.7	5	2.6	3½	3.4
GNP deflator	6½	6.8	4-5	3.3	4	3.8	3-3½	3.9
Capacity utilisation	0	−4½	2½	2½	2	—	½	½
Carry-over of central bank money growth[c]		3.1		5.4		4.3		4.8

a) Annual average.
b) Officially announced target: 8 per cent (end-1974 to end-1975).
c) Per cent deviation of December level in the preceding year from annual average.
Sources: Deutsche Bundesbank, Ministry of Economic Affairs, OECD Secretariat.

Monetary performance

The gradual transition to an intermediate quantity approach to monetary management was associated with a period of severe and prolonged monetary contraction, broadly lasting from the autumn of 1972 to the autumn of 1974. During this period, growth of the central bank money stock declined sharply. This was followed by a policy phase of cautious relaxation and, subsequently, active monetary easing as the recession intensified. Disregarding a short period of renewed tightening in 1976 (Chart B3)—which, however, was not intended to initiate a definite departure from the easy policy posture—easy monetary conditions have been maintained into 1979. This permitted a decline in key market interest rates to historically low levels, particularly putative "real" interest rates in the mortgage and consumer credit sectors, while growth of the central bank money stock exceeded the 8 per cent annual target levels by around one percentage point in both 1976 and 1977 an by 3½ percentage point in 1978 (Chart 5).

In view of the apparent instabilities in both the financial sector and price/wage behaviour, which gave rise to experimenting with the new quantity concept, the

12. Liquid assets held by the company sector relative to aggregate demand (GNP plus imports) developed as follows (in per cent):

	1970	1971	1972	1973	1974	1975	1976	1977	1978
Net liquidity ratio	1.9	2.1	2.5	1.3	0.3	1.3	1.3	1.7	2.0
Gross liquidity ratio	0.6	0.7	0.6	0.5	−0.9	2.0	0.4	1.2	1.4

Source: OECD Economic Outlook.

Chart 5. MONETARY MANAGEMENT AND INTEREST RATE TRENDS: GERMANY

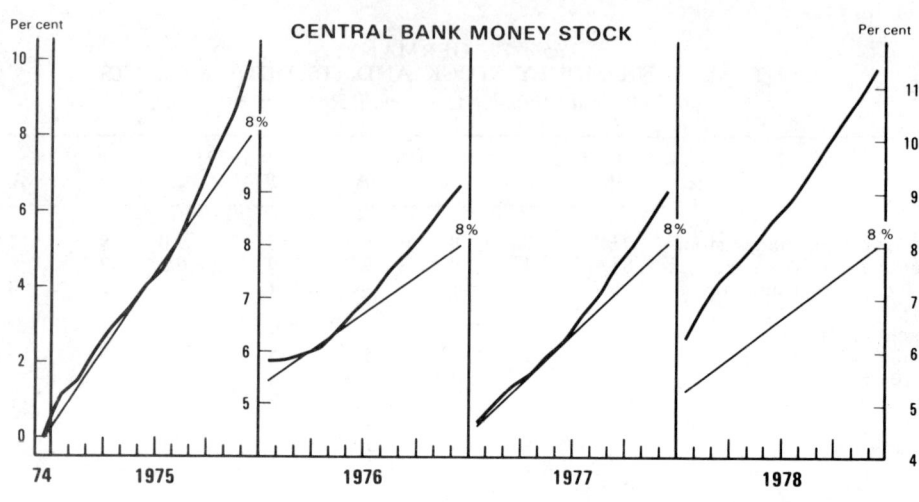
CENTRAL BANK MONEY STOCK

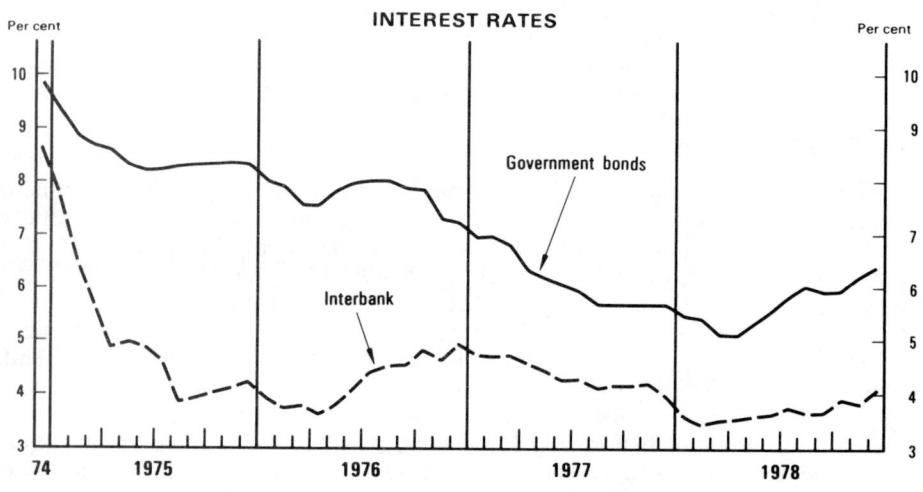
INTEREST RATES

CHANGES IN MAIN MONETARY POLICY INSTRUMENTS

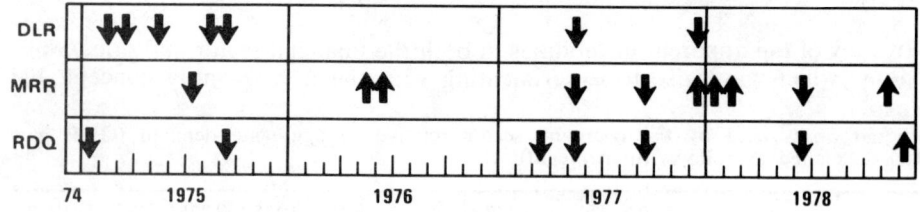

DLR: Discount and lombard rates.
MRR: Minimum reserve requirements.
RDQ: Rediscount quotas.

↑ Tightening
↓ Easing

Note: For sources and definitions see page 61.

authorities' strategy appears to have been reasonably successful in achieving monetary stabilisation goals. Although repeated "overshooting" of annual monetary growth targets has recently given rise to public concerns (see below), the yearly outcome for monetary growth during 1975-1977 was comparatively close to annual targets. At the same time, the establishing of a new basis for Bundesbank operations in the money market must be regarded as an achievement in its own right. More importantly, the advance in consumer prices was brought down from more than $8\frac{1}{2}$ per cent (non-adjusted) in the first half of 1974 to some $2\frac{1}{4}$ per cent in the second half of 1978, while wage settlements—which were well into double-digits in 1974[13]—were brought down to a $4\frac{1}{2}$ to 7 per cent range in 1978.

With stabilisation gains in the financial sphere and in the price/wage field being consolidated, increasing attention has been paid to technical aspects of the Bundesbank's implementation procedures and the possible implications for future inflation resulting from the perceived build-up of "excess liquidity" by end-1978. A potential source of complication is associated with present short-run operating procedures. While the Bundesbank broadly relies on a money-market based, "two-stage" control process resembling implementation procedures established at the Federal Reserve, information on the relevant relationships in the financial sector has been scarce. The authorities have thus had to "feel their way".[14] Moreover, lack of tradeable money market paper reduces the scope for flexible open market operations; but the Bundesbank was assisted in recent years through treasury cash and security transactions aiming at smooth management of banks' liquidity position. In addition, the authorities feel that variations in official lending rates are a flexible and powerful weapon for maintaining monetary control. The authorities have refrained from monetary "fine tuning"; they tended to react to monetary deviations with comparatively long response lags or tolerated such deviations deliberately while explaining the reasons to the general public. Although movements in the central bank money stock, which serves as a weighted proxy for M3, are reasonably close to M3 developments in the longer-run, the uneven representation of various money categories in the intermediate control variable adds to difficulties in day-to-day policy implementation.

Gradually emerging difficulties associated with heavy Bundesbank support in the government bond market in the autumn of 1975 (when open market purchases amounted to about DM $7\frac{1}{2}$ billion) served to stabilise the bond rate, and similar developments in the summer of 1978 (when the Bundesbank bought about DM 3 billion worth of government bonds) pointed to a potential conflict between maintenance of orderly securities market conditions and credible pursuit of monetary aggregate objectives. Disturbances arising from intervention commitments within EEC "snake" arrangements, which were conspicuously in evidence in early 1976 and the autumn of 1978, and the liquidity impact of heavy dollar support operations in 1977.Q4 and 1978 caused considerable complications for domestic liquidity management. Although the Bundesbank was able to broadly sterilise the impact of foreign capital inflows on bank reserves, the money supply was directly inflated due to huge inflows of funds through the non-bank sector. Combined with abnormal company liquidity preference or hoarding behaviour and the general uncertainties attached to predictability of velocity

---

13. Key metal workers settlements in 1974 foresaw effective increases in hourly rates of $14\frac{1}{2}$-15 per cent, incorporating accelerating increases in the last months of contract periods. This pointed to a disquieting rise in price expectations, which is often overlooked in international and time comparisons of recent German inflation performance.

14. Otmar Emminger: "The Role of the Central Banker", *Deutsche Bundesbank Press Excerpts*, N° 86, December 19, 1975, p. 3.

shifts, these external influences greatly contributed to the authorities' difficulties in monitoring monetary expansion. By international standards—and allowing for Germany's low rates of inflation and real growth—the acceleration in monetary growth since mid-1977 has been clearly exceptional, especially if recent developments in M1 are taken into account (Table 8). The authorities apparently gave priority to maintenance of easy credit market conditions in view of the depressed business situation and held out firmly against appreciation expectations in the exchange market.[15]

Table 8. RECENT DEVELOPMENTS IN MONETARY AGGREGATES IN GERMANY
Seasonally adjusted, annual rates, in per cent

	Average 1972-77	1977.Q4	1978.Q1	1978.Q2	1978.Q3	1978.Q4
Central Bank Money	8.6	10.6	13.3	9.4	9.6	13.6
Currency in Circulation	8.6	10.2	16.4	13.5	6.6	10.6
M1	8.8	10.9	19.6	8.5	10.2	13.0
M2	7.7	13.9	8.2	7.5	16.4	20.1
M3	9.5	11.7	7.3	7.5	13.8	14.8

Source: Deutsche Bundesbank.

Recent monetary debate in Germany has focussed on two perceived problem areas:

a) Publication of further statistical tests exploring the indicator quality of various monetary aggregates, their controllability, and the robustness of money demand relationships have led to the suggestion that alternative control procedures might be more efficient. A bank reserve variable, handled predominantly through open market operations, is often regarded as the superior short-run control instrument, while a number of observers would consider the narrow money stock as the most adequate policy lever at the macroeconomic level.

b) Public concern over accelerating monetary growth began to build up when the Bundesbank took no corrective action to counteract the rapid expansion of monetary aggregates since mid-1977. Whatever the economic justification of such concerns, the authorities have undoubtedly had to accept some loss of credibility in the eyes of an exceptionally inflation-conscious public, and the earlier signalling function associated with the Bundesbank's targeting practice may, at least temporarily, have ceased to be operative.

---

15. Historical evidence suggests that sterilisation efforts leaning permanently against market expectations could be self-defeating. Econometric studies covering German sterilisation experience up to the early 1970s point to "offset coefficients" of between 0.5 to as much as 0.9 relating liquidity absorbing domestic policy measures to "induced" capital inflows. See Manfred J.M. Neumann: "Offsetting Capital Flows", *Journal of Monetary Economics*, No. 4, (1978), pp. 131-142, and the references cited.

FRANCE

Among the provisions of the government programme for inflation control introduced in France in autumn 1976 was the announcement of a quantified target for the growth of money stock for 1977. On several earlier occasions, as a result of the use of direct credit control as a main instrument of monetary policy, the Banque de France had put limits on monetary growth.[16] These limits were not made public, however, and therefore did not have the character of explicit monetary targets; they were in fact normative projections used as a basis for calculating authorised or recommended rates of growth for bank credit. The main reason for announcing publicly a monetary growth target was the authorities' desire to strengthen the credibility of their anti-inflationary policy both at home and abroad. By explicitly limiting monetary expansion, the authorities also wanted to achieve greater stability in the conduct of monetary policy. Thus formulated, monetary policy is less oriented than hitherto towards fine tuning in the short term, but aims rather at moderating inflationary expectations and stabilising the exchange rate in the medium term.

The authorities consider the money supply broadly defined (M2) as the most appropriate aggregate for framing their objectives. Balances available for transactions are seen as not necessarily restricted to narrowly defined money (M1); moreover, idle balances, whether in the form of money or quasi-money, are considered able to be easily mobilised for use in transactions. The monetary authorities therefore prefer to control M2 rather than M1. As established for 1977 and the two subsequent years, the target for monetary growth features the following:

a) it is a single figure; in other words, no tolerance range for monetary growth is applied;
b) it is expressed as a change over the course of a year, with the rate of growth of the money supply calculated from the end of one year to the end of the next;
c) it constitutes an upper limit; the monetary authorities do not commit themselves necessarily to its attainment if actual monetary growth proves to be lower than foreseen.

Up to now, the maximum growth rates for the money supply—12.5 per cent for 1977, 12 per cent for 1978 and 11 per cent for 1979—have been fixed at levels near or slightly below the envisaged increase in nominal gross domestic product; these rates do not diverge from the moderate tendency observed in the course of 1976. In so doing, the authorities have aimed at roughly maintaining the domestic liquidity ratio—calculated as M2 over gross national expenditure—so as to gradually reduce the rate of inflation.

The application of formal limits to the growth of the money supply has not involved basic changes in the methods of monetary management. In fact, control of monetary expansion has continued to depend essentially on direct limitation on bank credit combined with some control of short-term interest rates. There are two main reasons for operating in this way. Firstly, the traditional structure of the French financial system and the depth of the money market are such that the central bank cannot easily ration its own credit to the banks[17] and hence the quantity of reserve money (monetary base) in circulation. Indeed, commercial banks are largely dependent on the central bank to cover their reserve money requirements, and, in order to prevent sharp pressure on money market rates,

---

16. See *"Monetary Policy in France"*, OECD, Monetary Studies Series, 1974.
17. For further details on this point, see the above-quoted OECD study.

the central bank normally provides the banks with the means of covering their liquidity needs. Secondly, although the central bank can closely influence market interest rates, its action in this field is limited by external and internal considerations: exchange rate behaviour, structure of the financial system and encouragement of investment. The result is that the monetary authorities are not in a position to effectively control monetary expansion directly by controlling bank liquidity or indirectly by operating through interest rates.[18] They are therefore obliged to operate on money creation at the retail level. Since bank credit to enterprises and individuals constitutes by far the largest source of money creation, it is on the rationing of this category of credit that the regulation of monetary expansion mainly depends. Thus, since the end of 1972, the monetary authorities have announced monthly norms for the increase in lending by the banks and finance companies, which, if exceeded, require additional reserves at steeply progressive rates on total outstanding credit distributed by these institutions.

The consistency of the monetary growth target with the objective for bank credit expansion involves close surveillance over the other sources of money creation, i.e. bank claims on the Treasury and the official exchange reserves.[19] In this respect, the authorities have resorted to a strict limitation of Treasury financing through the banking system—financing the public sector deficit mainly by non-bank saving—and to a controlled floating of the franc—financing balance-of-payments deficits by capital inflows. To these ends, the authorities have relied, *inter alia,* on long-term Government borrowing from households influenced by tax incentives. Furthermore, their attention to exchange rate stability has led to the maintenance of relatively high interest rates and the encouragement of borrowing in foreign capital markets by public and private enterprises.

As Chart 6 shows, monetary growth in 1977 was roughly consistent with the 12.5 per cent limit fixed for that year. With the money stock consequently increasing in line with nominal gross domestic product, the domestic liquidity ratio remained fairly stable in 1977, in conformity with the authorities' intentions. However, this result was achieved on the basis of a growth rate of real output and a rate of inflation different from those which had been officially envisaged. While the increase in volume of GDP was less than foreseen (3 per cent instead of 4.6 per cent), the rise in the GDP price deflator turned out to be higher (8.9 per cent instead of 8.2 per cent). Although these trends were discernable in the course of the year, the authorities did not consider it necessary to lower the target for monetary growth since, given the slackening of economic activity, the limit fixed seemed sufficiently restrictive. During 1978 the growth of M2 ran slightly ahead of the 12 per cent objective for the year as a whole, reflecting mainly an increase in official foreign exchange reserves and larger Government financing requirements. The growth of nominal GDP was also somewhat stronger than anticipated with, as in 1977, a lower increase in real output and a higher rate of inflation (3.3 and 9.9 per cent respectively compared to projected 4.3 and 7.9 per cent).

---

18. It may be added that, given the low interest rate elasticity of demand for credit, a policy of manipulating rates to control monetary expansion is less effective in a period of rapid inflation such as France has known in recent years.
19. When calculating the targets for 1977 and 1978, foreign exchange transactions and Treasury financing were assumed neutral. In 1979, in view of trends actually observed and the difficulty of forecasting precisely changes in the money supply counterparts more exposed to exogenous influences, the authorities decided to abandon this assumption; then, they introduced some flexibility by fixing the norms for bank credit expansion every 6 months instead of annually, so as to be able to adjust bank credit restrictions according to trends observed in the other sources of money creation.

Chart 6. MONETARY MANAGEMENT AND INTEREST RATE TRENDS: FRANCE

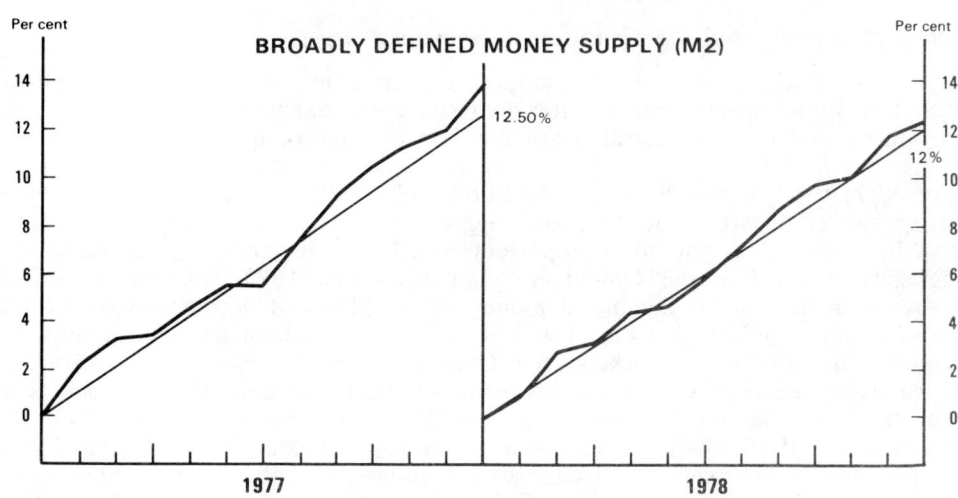

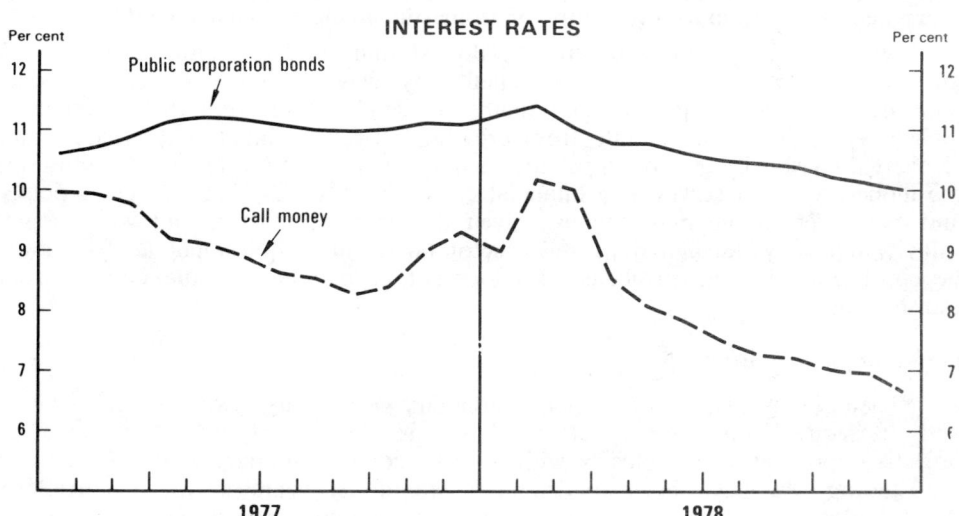

TREND IN BANK LENDING SUBJECT TO CEILINGS
Indices, end December preceding year   100

	1977				1978			
	March	June	September	December	March	June	September	December
Main banks								
— Levels authorised without supplementary reserve requirements	99	101	102	105	99	101	102	105
— Levels actually reached (1)	98.2	99.7	99	104.1	98.6	98.8	98.4	107.2
Other banks								
— Levels authorised without supplementary reserve requirements	101	104	105	108	101	104	105	108
— Levels actually reached (1)	100.3	102.9	101.2	107.1	100.2	101.7	101.7	108.9

1. Allowing for the use of previous undistributed credit margins.

Note: For sources and definitions see page 61.

UNITED KINGDOM

Policy philosophy and the transition to monetary targets

In connection with 1968 standby arrangements with the International Monetary Fund, specific ceilings for domestic credit expansion (DCE) had been introduced that had concentrated attention on the role of quantity variables and projections in the conduct of U.K. monetary policy. Financial reform measures adopted in the framework of "Competition and Credit Control" in 1971, which put greater emphasis on the monetary aggregates in domestic policy formulation, may be regarded as the most important initial step towards explicit monetary aggregates control in the United Kingdom. By late 1973, maintenance of a desired growth rate for the broad money stock (M3) had become an important informal policy objective. Faced with a build-up of destabilising expectations in financial and exchange markets, the Chancellor of the Exchequer—with the active encouragement of the central bank—publicly announced a 12 per cent growth target for M3 for the fiscal year 1976-1977 in July 1976. Starting in December 1976 when a stand-by arrangement was concluded with the IMF, priority was again given to DCE control; however, with external conditions improving, adherence to targets published for sterling M3 for subsequent fiscal years became an important feature of domestic financial management.[20]

With respect to policy practices followed since mid-1976, monetary targets are seen as providing immediate benefits by way of improved expectations: published monetary objectives and their successful implementation are expected to help keep the exchange rate from creating exogenous inflation pressures, and to avert domestically generated inflation surges in the medium term. In addition, the monetary target serves as a financial consistency "check" on budgetary policy and overall economic management: given the monetary target, and with money velocity not fully flexible, the public sector borrowing requirement (PSBR) must be consistent with the projected development of national income and external transactions.

Policy implementation

The circumstances under which a monetary growth target was first announced, and subsequent targeting practices, have, in fact, associated the monetary objective approach rather closely with overall economic management. Objectives for sterling M3 have been made public for fiscal years in the Chancellor's April budget speeches. Seen in this context, the announced monetary target, at least implicitly, provides a macroeconomic frame of reference for the financing side of the budget, external objectives, and the government's intentions in the field of prices and incomes policies. Allowing for external financing transactions as a potential "wedge" between money and domestic credit, the broad money stock—which represents the bulk of the banking system's liabilities—can be systematically linked to DCE, the indicator used in establishing financial commitments with the IMF. Given financing requirements of the budget, the authorities' ability to meet these by the sales of debt to the non-bank public, and net external transactions, the residual quantitative counterpart of the broad money stock is largely determined by sterling bank lending to the private sector. The deposit base affecting the latter can be influenced through interest rates and

---

20. Sterling M3 excludes deposits held by U.K. residents denominated in currencies other than sterling. DCE equals sterling M3 plus increases in non-deposit bank liabilities and external and foreign-currency financing.

ceiling techniques, e.g. the "corset",[21] and exchange controls. Sterling M3 would thus suggest itself as a dominant domestic control expedient because of its plausible indicator value in the context of government financial commitments, but also on technical grounds, since all its major counterparts in the banking system's balance sheet are, in some degree, in the authorities' control.

The authorities implement monetary objectives mainly by:

a) manipulating as far as possible the treasury-bill proportion (mostly absorbed by the banking system) and bond-financing share (placed mainly with the non-bank public) of the public sector borrowing requirement;
b) consistently influencing money market rates, and,
c) in conditions where there is a risk of excessive bank lending to the private sector, reactivating the "corset".

Since the authorities are hesitant to sell government bonds aggressively and/or adjust money market rates excessively at short intervals, large-scale resort to "residual" bill financing through the banking system has repeatedly led to short-run monetary "overshooting", raising simultaneously banks' reserve assets among which treasury bills play a prominent role. In such circumstances the recorded increase in money supply growth may be associated simply with an increase in deposits of financial institutions awaiting long term investment, and as such the increase may carry no implications for future output or inflation. But such increases have sometimes created adverse interest and exchange rate expectations; to regain control of the aggregates, the authorities were forced into sharp upwards adjustments in money market rates in order to create the "bullish" conditions in the bond market needed for large gilt-edged sales, or imposition of the "corset" as in late 1976 and mid-1978.[22]

In order to reduce these potential sources of financial disturbances, proposals for instrumental reform have been advanced and actively discussed:

a) Retaining the essential characteristics of the present system, the authorities have been encouraged by a number of outside experts to permit more spontaneous adjustments in long-term interest rates, expand the use of unofficial bond "tap" stocks to facilitate active gilt sales, issue index-linked bonds, or sell government bonds on a tender basis. In order to mitigate the impact of expectations of rising interest rates on gilt-edged sales, the authorities introduced floating rate bonds in the first half of 1977.
b) More fundamental proposals have included abandoning of the reserve asset quality of treasury bills and active management of bank cash reserves through open market operations corresponding to practices in other major countries. Moreover, given the apparent relative stability of demand relationships for M1 (see page 26), the narrow money stock might well be regarded as a potential supplementary target variable.

Policy performance

Determined efforts to contain the rate of monetary expansion, which the authorities had undertaken before official targets were announced, were remarkably

---

21. The "corset" serves to control the rate at which banks' interest-bearing eligible liabilities expand. Banks exceeding official limits are required to place non-interest bearing supplementary special deposits with the Bank of England. The implicit profit disincentives are made sharply progressive, acting effectively as a credit ceiling.
22. Predictability of the authorities' reaction has led financial markets to expect "lumpiness" in interest rates and gilt-edged sales as a more or less regular feature of target-oriented monetary management.

successful until early 1976. The rate of growth of M3 was stabilised at an annual rate of about 10 per cent from around mid-1974 and the financial system seemed to have adapted to the Bank of England's policy of moderating M3 growth. However, since late spring of 1976, there have been considerable short run fluctuations in monetary growth as well as in interest rates. This can, at least partly, be attributed to market expectations relating to general economic trends, the perceived stance of government policies, exchange rate disturbances and interest rate developments abroad. In addition, extreme sensitivity of financial and exchange markets to short-term deviations in monetary aggregates, as well as seeming conflict between budget financing requirements and published monetary objectives, appear to have contributed to volatile behaviour of interest rates, monetary aggregates, and the exchange rate (Charts A5 and B5).

The overall stabilisation gains achieved since the autumn of 1976 are impressive, although it may be difficult to establish precise evidence of the specific contribution of cautious monetary management to more acceptable exchange rate and inflation trends. A less welcome aspect has been the somewhat uneven manner in which these achievements have come about. And since the spring of 1978, the authorities have been facing pressures which, albeit in a much less dramatic way, bear some resemblance to the financial imbalances experienced two years ago. Broadly speaking, monetary developments over the period under review may be characterised by distinguishing three major policy episodes (Chart 7):

a) *Late 1976-autumn 1977*. With financial markets responding favourably to restrictive monetary and fiscal action, successfull completion of the IMF stand-by, and consolidation arrangements among central banks for volatile sterling balances, a definite return of confidence in the future of sterling led to a dramatic turnaround in financial conditions. Partly mirroring heavy capital inflows and the resulting expansionary impact on domestic liquidity, the Minimum Lending Rate was brought down from 15 per cent (end-November 1976) to 5 per cent (mid-October 1977), and the effective rate of sterling appreciated by about 9 percentage points between early November 1976 and mid-January 1977. Large-scale sales of gilt-edged securities to the public enabled the authorities to keep domestic credit expansion clearly below the DCE ceiling, while sterling M3—following significant "under-shooting" in early 1977—remained well within the 9-13 per cent target range.

b) *October 1977-spring 1978*. In the face of continuing capital inflows, which began to reflect the weakness of the dollar rather than inherent strength of sterling, the authorities' attempt to preserve simultaneously a competitive exchange rate, low interest rate levels and the control of monetary aggregates proved to be unsustainable. At the end of October the authorities let the exchange rate adjust upwards; this made possible and upward adjustment in the Minimum Lending Rate by two percentage points in late November in order to counter an acceleration in domestically generated monetary growth. The effective rate of sterling appreciated by around 5 percentage points over the period end-October 1977 to early February 1978, and sterling M3 moved outside the outer tolerance range between mid-October 1977 and mid-March 1978.

c) *April-1978—end-1978*. By the end of the first quarter of 1978, the effective sterling rate had depreciated by about 4 percentage points and, given the persisting strength in monetary growth, the authorities became concerned about a build-up of adverse expectations and possible excessive downward adjustment of the exchange rate. Fiscal easing incor-

Chart 7. MONETARY MANAGEMENT AND INTEREST RATE TRENDS: UNITED KINGDOM

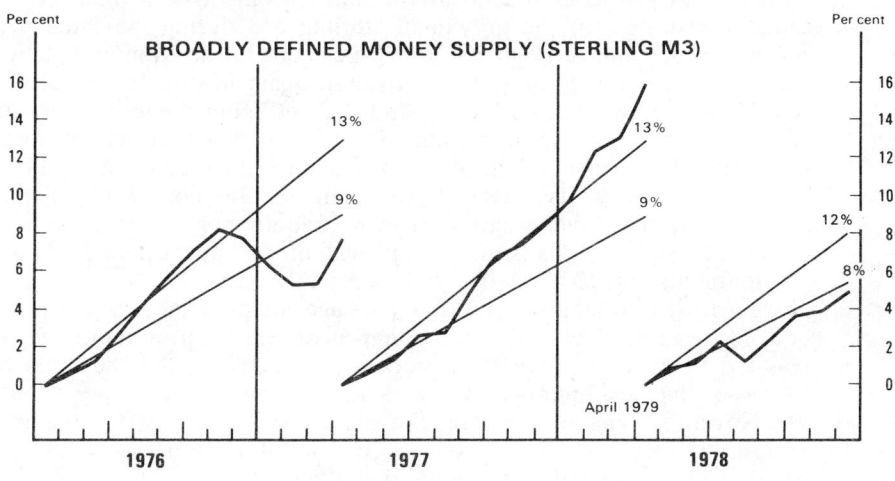

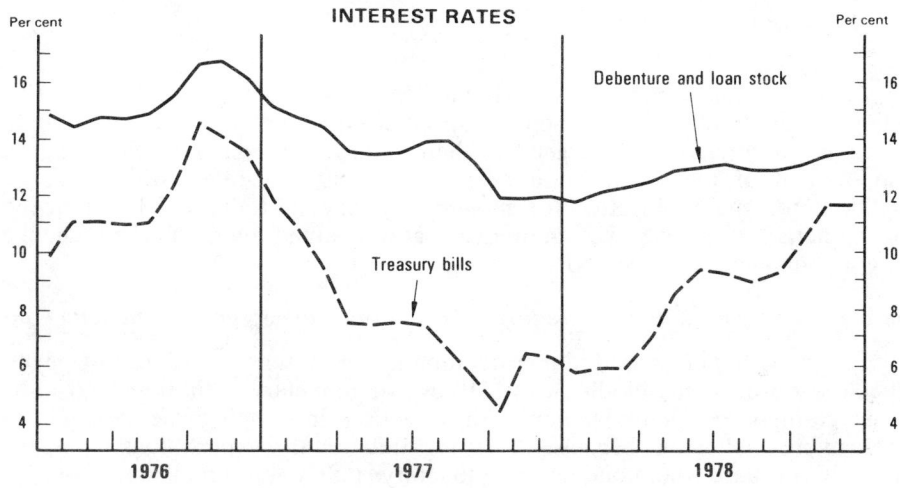

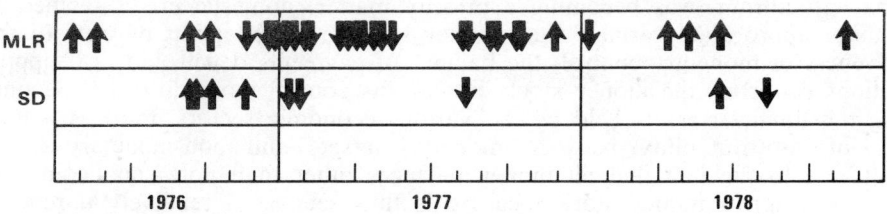

MLR: Minimum lending rate.
SD: Special deposits required from banks and finance houses (completed by special supplementary deposits - *corset* - from November 1976 to August 1977 and again as from June 1978).

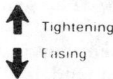 Tightening
Easing

Note: For sources and definitions see page 61.

porated in the budget for the fiscal year 1978 (twelve months ending April 1979) was combined with the announcement of a tight 8-12 per cent target range for the growth of sterling M3 during the same period and a one percentage point rise to 7½ per cent in the Minimum Lending Rate. The official lending rate was raised again in three steps to 10 per cent by the second week of June, and "corset" controls were reintroduced. These measures took account of a rise in North American interest rates and of adverse financial market sentiment which was influenced by persisting monetary "overshooting" and doubts concerning the compatibility of the government borrowing requirement (further increased in the course of parliamentary approval of the budget) and monetary commitments for 1978-1979. Persistent increases in U.S. interest rates along with the dollar stabilisation package adopted in early November, and uncertainties about the maintenance of wage norms, both of which resulted in an upward drift in market interest rates, led the authorities to raise the Minimum Lending Rate sharply to 12½ per cent on 9th November and to maintain the 8-12 per cent target for the twelve months to October 1979. At the end of 1978 monetary growth was running at a rate consistent with the official targets.

ITALY

Following loans contracted with the IMF and the EEC in 1974-1975, the Italian monetary authorities adopted a specific monetary aggregate (total domestic credit) as an intermediate target for their policy. This led to the progressive abandonment of the stabilization of long-term interest rates, which was for a long time the main objective for monetary policy in Italy.[23] The choice of a new monetary objective was, moreover, accompanied by a marked change in monetary management methods.

The choice of total domestic credit as the intermediate target for monetary policy

Faced with very rapid domestic inflation and serious balance-of-payments difficulties towards the middle of the 1970s, the monetary authorities had to apply an increasingly restrictive policy. Since action influencing the cost of credit was proving ineffective because of strong inflationary expectations, it appeared necessary to base the conduct of monetary policy on credit rationing. The choice of domestic credit as a monetary target, in preference to some measure of the money stock, was made for two reasons. First, since the restoration of external equilibrium was becoming a priority matter, domestic credit seemed to be a more appropriate variable than money stock from the point of view of the effectiveness of monetary control; the balance-of-payments deficit and lira-support operations disturbed the money stock, making its control more difficult. Second, among the financial assets held by the various economic sectors, there is a high degree of substitutability between monetary assets and non-monetary assets (mainly due to the fact that all money balances other than notes and coins are interest bearing); a money stock measure is thus seen as a relatively unreliable guide for monetary policy.[24] Two other factors explain why the monetary

---

23. See on this point, *The Role of Monetary Policy in Demand Management: The experience of six major countries*, OECD, Monetary Studies Series, 1975.
24. In this connection, it can be noted that econometric studies show a certain instability in the demand for money in Italy. See on this point J. Boughton, "The Demand for Money in Major OECD countries", *OECD Economic Outlook, Occasional Studies*, No. 24, January 1979.

authorities chose to formulate their policy with reference to total domestic credit rather than simply to bank credit. In the first place, given the close relationships existing between the activities of the banks and those of the special credit institutions, bank credit and non-bank credit are in practice largely interchangeable. In the second place, the bond market plays an important role in the financing of the economy. Thus, the domestic credit variable selected as target includes, in addition to the credit distributed by the banks, loans made by the special credit institutions, government and private bond issues, and net indebtedness of the state sector.[25]

The target for total domestic credit is calculated on the basis of annual forecasts of financial flows concerning the assets and liabilities of the main financial sectors (Treasury, banks and special credit institutions), the sources and uses of the money supply, and the instruments of the capital markets. These financial forecasts are made with the help of the econometric model of the Bank of Italy,[26] on the basis of anticipated trends in real economic variables. Consequently, the target for total domestic credit resulting from these forecasts corresponds to a given projection of economic developments; any modification in this projection would cause a revision of the target.

Changes in monetary management methods

Prior to the introduction of a target for total domestic credit, monetary management in Italy operated mainly through control of monetary base creation.[27] In doing this, the monetary authorities tended to control the supply of bank credit indirectly by influencing bank reserves. This method of operating proved to be impracticable in the early 1970s since, because of the important financing of the Treasury deficit by the central bank,[28] control of the monetary base, and hence the regulation of bank reserves, became increasingly difficult. In these conditions, from 1973 onwards, it appeared necessary to control bank credit directly. Two new monetary policy instruments were introduced, one designed to limit the increase in banks' assets (ceiling on bank loans) and the other aiming at influencing the composition of those assets in the framework of a selective orientation of credit (banks being required to invest a certain proportion of their total deposits and, subsequently, of the increase in their total deposits, in the form of long-term securities). By acting in this way, the monetary authorities ensured that Treasury borrowing was principally financed by the banks rather than by the central bank and encouraged the deepening of the interbank market for government short-term securities. In parallel with this, and in accordance with conditions on the loans contracted with the EEC, a strict ceiling was put on monetary base creation for financing the Treasury deficit.

Since the objective aimed at by the monetary authorities involves a rationing of bank and non-bank financing, quantitative limits were also put on the expansion of total domestic credit. Compliance with these limits was ensured by means of specific ceilings on bank credit and strict surveillance of long-term securities issues, which constitute the bulk of the resources available to the special credit institutions to finance their loans. While centering their policy on direct credit control, the monetary authorities nevertheless tended to improve their other

25. For a more detailed definition, see note (2) of Chart 8.
26. Cf. F. Cotula and R. Masera, "Some considerations on the Banca d'Italia's Approach to the Forecasting of Financial Flows", Paper presented at the Meeting of Technicians of Central Banks of the American Continent, San Carlos de Bariloche, November 1977.
27. On the modalities of this control, see the above-quoted OECD Study.
28. This situation resulted from the rapid increase in Treasury requirements and the difficulties of placing issues of public securities on the long-term capital market.

instruments for indirect action. Thus, by encouraging the development of the market for short-term Treasury bonds, the central bank aimed at broadening the field of its open-market intervention for the regulation of the monetary base. Moreover, in contrast to its attitude in the past, the central bank has been making frequent and substantial changes in its lending rates[29] in order to make short-term interest rates much more flexible. In addition, in order to have better control over bank liquidity, the composition and method of calculating compulsory reserves against bank deposits were changed at the beginning of 1975. Another important means of action on bank liquidity resulted from the introduction of an import deposits scheme in 1974, and again in 1976. In fact, by compelling importers to deposit in a non-interest bearing account with the Bank of Italy a fixed percentage of the value of certain categories of products purchased abroad, the system had the result of freezing temporarily a considerable proportion of domestic liquidity.

Conclusions from recent monetary experience

The governmental stabilization programmes implemented during the years 1974 to 1978, in agreement with the IMF and (or) the EEC, aimed at achieving two basic economic goals—reduction of domestic inflation and restoration of external equilibrium—by adhering to intermediate monetary and budgetary targets (limits to total domestic credit expansion, public sector deficit and growth of public expenditures). In the following paragraphs economic and monetary trends since 1974 are examined to see how far these objectives have been achieved.

As the few indicators presented in Chart A6 show, the situation of the Italian economy gradually improved in 1974-1975 after the aggravation of the internal and external imbalances which followed the increases in the prices of oil and commodities: but, as in the other major OECD countries, the reduction in the external deficit and in the rate of inflation was obtained at the cost of a serious recession marked by a sudden, steep fall in production and a rise in unemployment. The recovery in economic activity, which started at the end of 1975 and continued through 1976, caused a new deterioration in the current account balance and strong pressures on the lira exchange rate. This triggered off an inflationary spiral—the depreciation of the lira leading to an increase in domestic prices and, through indexation, in wages—prompting the decision of the Italian authorities, in autumn 1976, to tighten up the monetary and fiscal austerity programme. This was followed, in the course of 1977 and 1978, by an improvement in the balance of payments on current account and a reduction in the rate of inflation which went beyond the targets agreed with the IMF and EEC;[30] at the same time, official exchange reserves increased and the lira exchange rate steadied. These favourable results were, however, accompanied by a new slowdown in activity until the third quarter of 1978, with a prolonged decline in investment and a worsening of the employment situation.

As regards the achievement of the monetary target, Chart 8 shows that the expansion of total domestic credit (in terms of flows) exceeded the ceilings

---

29. Discount rate and rate of advances on securities.
30. From April 1977 to March 1978, the current balance showed a surplus of some 1 200 billion lire compared with an IMF target of 500 billion surplus. As for the inflation rate, measured by the rise in consumer prices based on the reference index for the calculation of cost of living allowances, this reached—in terms of change during the same period—somewhat more than 12 per cent as against an IMF target of about 13 per cent. Over the whole year 1978, the current account surplus amounted roughly to 5 400 billion lire compared with an EEC target of 3 000 billion lire while the rise in consumer prices—from the fourth quarter of 1977 to the fourth quarter of 1978—reached 11.5 per cent against an EEC target of 14 per cent.

Chart 8. TOTAL DOMESTIC CREDIT AND TREASURY FINANCING IN ITALY
Cumulative flows, end-month, billion lire

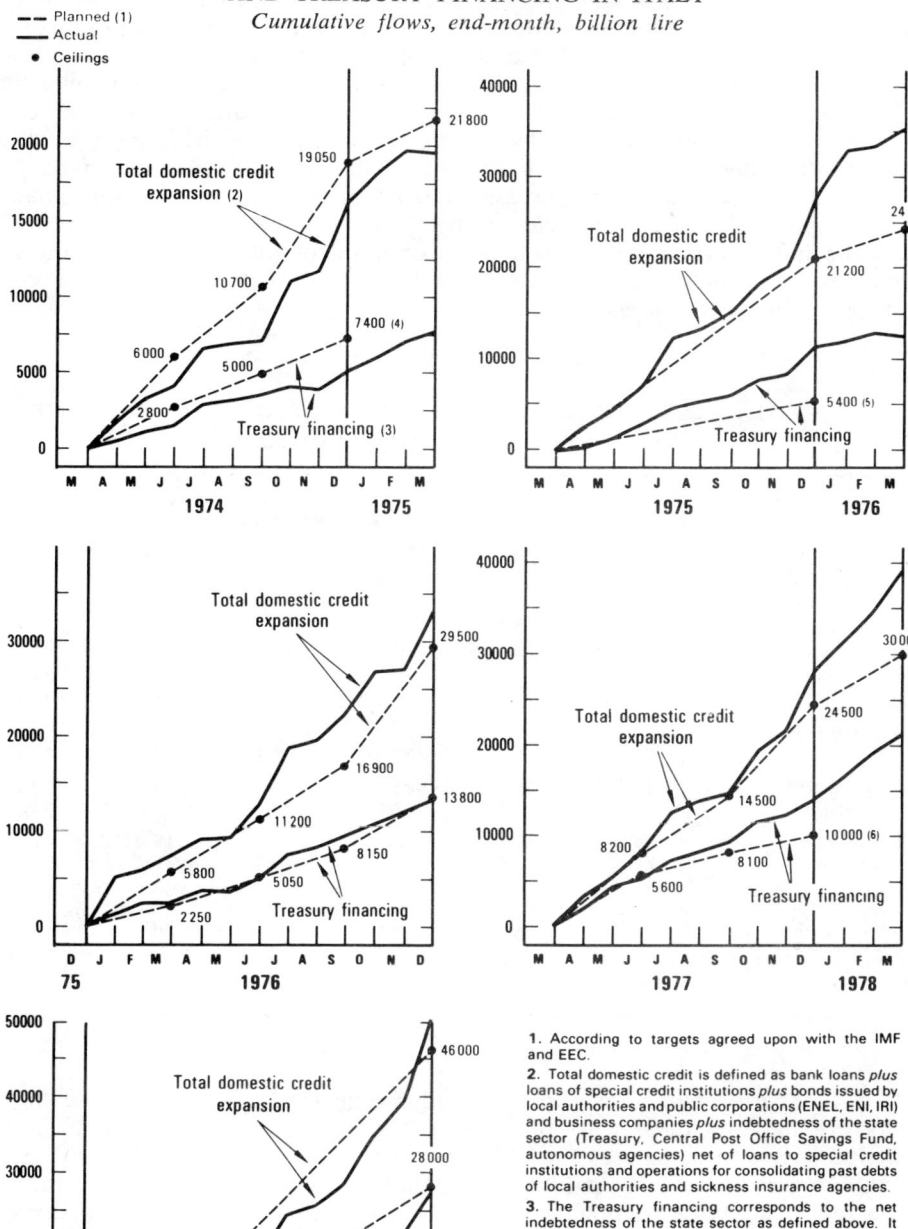

1. According to targets agreed upon with the IMF and EEC.
2. Total domestic credit is defined as bank loans *plus* loans of special credit institutions *plus* bonds issued by local authorities and public corporations (ENEL, ENI, IRI) and business companies *plus* indebtedness of the state sector (Treasury, Central Post Office Savings Fund, autonomous agencies) net of loans to special credit institutions and operations for consolidating past debts of local authorities and sickness insurance agencies.
3. The Treasury financing corresponds to the net indebtedness of the state sector as defined above. It reflects the deficit of the state budget as well as portions of the deficits of other public bodies (local authorities, National Provident Fund, Fund for the South and autonomous agencies).
4. Corresponds to the ceiling for the year 1974 of 9,200 billion lire less the outturn of 1,800 billion lire in the first quarter.
5. Corresponds to the ceiling for the year 1975 of 8,000 billion lire less the outturn of 2,600 billion lire in the first quarter.
6. Corresponds to the ceiling for the year 1977 of 13,100 billion lire less the outturn of 3,100 billion lire in the first quarter.

Sources: Bank of Italy and IMF.

fixed for the periods covering April 1975 to March 1976, the whole year 1976, April 1977 to March 1978, and the whole year 1978 respectively, whereas it had remained below the ceiling for the period from April 1974 to March 1975. Similar trends are revealed in Table 9, in which the targets for total domestic credit are presented as growth rates over the calendar year. One explanation for the greater than expected growth of total domestic credit in 1975 and 1977 was the financing of the increasing borrowing requirements of the Treasury, whose deficit substantially exceeded the limits which had been fixed.[31] In fact, this situation gave rise to a steep increase in bank claims on the Treasury mainly because of purchases of public securities by the commercial banks. During 1976 and in the latter part of 1978, the faster expansion of total domestic credit was more the result of an acceleration in bank and non-bank credit to the private sector associated with the economic recovery.

Table 9. ITALY: MONETARY AGGREGATES AND NOMINAL PRODUCT
Percentage changes over previous year

	Monetary Base	Money Supply (M2)	Bank Loans[a]	Banks' Purchases of Securities[b]	Total Domestic Credit	Nominal GDP
1974 - planned	..	18.0	..	..	19.0[c]	15.0
- actual	15.4	15.5	20.8	31.2	16.5	23.3
1975 - planned	..	..	..	..	18.0[c]	18.0
- actual	18.6	23.5	17.7	42.3	22.4	13.1
1976 - planned	..	..	..	..	17.8	22.1
- actual	16.4	21.1	23.2	16.6	19.8	24.9
1977 - planned	17.0	19.0	16.0	..	16.0	22.2
- actual	18.9	21.9	14.9	47.4	17.8	21.1
1978 - planned	18.6	19.6	..	..	19.3	17.1
- actual	24.3	22.6	11.9	30.3	21.2	16.3

a) Including operations for consolidating past debts of local authorities and sickness insurance agencies.
b) Excluding Treasury bills included in compulsory reserves and securities acquired in counterpart of consolidating operations.
c) Partly estimated from flows data.
Source: Bank of Italy and OECD Secretariat.

If the performance regarding total domestic credit is compared with the results obtained in respect to the balance of payments and inflation, it can be seen that over three periods (in 1975 and, even more clearly, in 1977 and 1978) the final objectives of the stabilization policy were achieved overall, although the degree of credit restriction proved to be less severe than planned. Conversely, in 1976, economic instability increased whereas, if one takes into account the speeding up of inflation, the real contraction of credit seems to have been relatively more pronounced. Thus, the effects of credit rationing appeared in the event to be rather imprecise. However, it is also possible that the impact lags

---

31. The other ceilings for the overall public sector deficit and the increase in public expenditure laid down for 1977 were also exceeded. Moreover, sizeable operations to consolidate the debt of certain public bodies occurred towards the end of 1977, which had the effect of increasing considerably the amount of bank lending.

of credit policy may in practice have been significantly different from those which had been anticipated at the time when the targets were set.

Having resulted mainly from a rapid increase in bank credit to the public sector, the overshooting of the targets for total domestic credit was reflected to some extent in monetary expansion (Table 9). The increase in purchases of Treasury bonds by the commercial banks tended to exert an expansionary effect on the money supply broadly defined (M2) in two ways:

— directly (as in 1975 and 1977), as a result of the expansion of total bank assets;
— indirectly (as in 1976) as a result of monetary base creation due to the repurchase by the central bank—through open market operations—of Treasury bonds held by the banks.

Overall, however, monetary expansion proved in the event to be close to the growth of nominal product except in 1975 and, to a lesser extent, in 1978. The building up of a considerable excess liquidity during 1975 facilitated the massive capital outflows which occured in the last months of that year and the beginning of 1976, thus contributing to the development of downward pressures on the lira exchange rate.

CANADA

The philosophy and implementation of monetary targeting

In November 1975, in a widely publicized move, the Canadian monetary authorities shifted their policy orientation from the stabilization of credit conditions to the stabilization of longer-run monetary growth. Canada was led to adopt this approach by the emergence of inflation as an overriding problem by the mid-1970s. The country had weathered the 1974-1975 world recession due to its energy independence, its accommodative policies, and strength in its resource-based investments. In addition, its position as an exporter of a number of basic commodities whose prices had risen strongly in earlier years had generated rapid increases in nominal income. The Bank of Canada found itself accommodating high nominal income growth as pressures for wage increases spread through an economy largely shielded from real income drain to oil producing countries. Moreover, Canadian ties to the U.S. economy, in the context of a policy that sought to stabilise relative interest rates, proved inflationary. With the Canadian dollar remaining fairly stable in terms of its U.S. counterpart, Canada could not avoid "importing" U.S. goods price inflation. On the financial side, the tie to U.S. financial conditions contributed to an "explosion" of Canadian M1 growth by the first quarter of 1975. As U.S. interest rates dropped sharply from their 1974 "credit crunch" levels, short-term capital movements into Canadian financial instruments soared to unprecedented levels, putting strong downward pressure on Canadian interest rates. In general, the Canadian authorities acquiesced to this decline, lowering Bank Rate in January 1975 and taking the opportunity to continue their policy of a gradual reduction in the secondary reserve requirement. The Bank of Canada absorbed a large proportion of the treasury bills released by these moves. Resistance to the interest rate decline, and its monetary consequences, may also have been tempered by a desire to avoid any exchange rate appreciation, given the sharp decline in the trade balance that had occurred in 1974. In consequence the money supply continued to grow at exceptionally high rates.

Under these influences, price pressures showed less of a tendency to improve in Canada than its trading partners, and inflationary expectations, if anything worsened: the average annual increase in wage settlements steadily mounted throughout 1974 and into 1975, reaching nearly 20 per cent in the second quarter (Chart A7). At this point, an anti-inflation policy was assembled which principally involved wage and price controls and a determined monetary aggregates policy by the Bank of Canada. As it began to be implemented in mid-1975, the most immediate result was an abrupt divergence between U.S. and Canadian interest rate trends that persisted until 1978.

The policy stance adopted by the Bank of Canada had a very long time horizon by usual standards. The Bank specifically rejected a "credit crunch" policy to lower monetary growth rates quickly to levels consistent with much lower inflation as unacceptably disruptive to the domestic economy. Instead, it aimed to starve inflation gradually over the medium-term, slowly bringing monetary growth down to levels consistent with price stability; the authorities were therefore prepared to establish monetary growth targets at rates slightly under the monetary expansion implied by a policy that would fully accommodate nominal income growth. The implied policy "gradualism" thus sought to minimize the cost of winding-down inflation while contributing to the fastest possible amelioration of inflation expectations. The Bank specifically and publicly recognised that the emphasis on monetary aggregates would require a tolerance of greater potential variability in interest and exchange rates than had previously been the case; and it was stressed that fiscal policy would have to be counter-cyclically tuned if undesirable swings in interest rates and exchange rate were to be avoided. Credit conditions thus virtually ceased to be regarded as a key policy indicator. Interest rates were to be used as an instrument to achieve monetary growth targets, leading, rather than lagging, the preferred intermediate monetary target. The authorities' willingness to countenance large swings in U.S.-Canadian interest rate differentials, and its repeated commitment to an essentially freely floating exchange rate, should thus be seen as an integral element of the basic policy philosophy. Nevertheless, experience in the latter part of the period under review, showed that in Canada, as in other countries, extreme exchange rate movements could force temporary suspension of the fundamental policy approach in order to resist further currency pressures.

The Bank of Canada's policy approach is based on its empirical conclusion that a fairly stable relationship exists between M1 and nominal income over the long run. In addition, the demand for M1 is thought to be predictably related to the level of the short-term interest rates over which the Bank exercises sufficient control. Canadian policy, then, amounts to looking at M1 as an intermediate indicator of nominal income growth. The technique of implementation begins with a notional range for future nominal income growth that embodies a gradual reduction in the rate of inflation and a reasonable expansion of real output. Based on the fairly stable relationship between nominal income and M1, a target band for growth in M1 is set which will accommodate this increase in income at unchanged interest rates; in the inflation environment of recent years, this has involved a continuing gradual deceleration in the targeted rates of monetary growth. In practice, growth of M1 above the target range is seen as evidence that nominal income is expanding in an undesirably inflationary manner, suggesting that interest rates must rise in order to maintain the monetary objectives. The converse goes for sluggish monetary growth. The Bank of Canada actively resists such monetary trends by putting upward or downward pressure on short-term interest rates. Through a normal demand-for-money process, these interest rate changes affect the money stock, in effect temporarily moving money velocity from its long-term trend. Nominal income then adjusts to restore the more normal relationship between GNP and M1.

Policy performance

Monetary policy performance over the period since the adoption of aggregate objectives in 1975 can be broken into three periods:

a) *Mid-1975—late 1976.* During this period the authorities were principally concerned with getting excessive nominal income growth under control. Very high rates of growth of M1 were recorded throughout 1975 (the quarterly average was an annual rate of some 20 per cent), the result of accelerating inflation and a quick recovery from the very mild recession of 1974. In addition, the Bank of Canada had actively absorbed government debt through mid-1975, allowing Canadian interest rates to fall with U.S. rates, perhaps in part out of concern over the high exchange rate experienced in 1974. As the authorities moved to an active anti-inflation posture, Bank of Canada purchases of new government debt were significantly reduced, and the Bank rate was raised a total of $1\frac{1}{4}$ percentage points in two steps, to reach $9\frac{1}{2}$ per cent in March 1976. These measures resulted in an immediate and sharp decline in monetary growth that persisted throughout 1976, facilitating the Bank of Canada's decision to lower the M1 range in the fourth quarter of 1976 (Chart 9). With the income policy programme beginning to take effect as well—particularly on wages—nominal income growth began to decelerate by the second quarter of 1976. In the second half of that year, the economic growth stagnated.

b) *Late 1976—early 1978.* With unemployment rising and the Canadian dollar back at its 1974 peak, with new wage settlements yielding annualised increases of under 8 per cent and with M1 growth falling well below the floor of the gradually reduced objective range, the Bank of Canada began to encourage credit expansion in late 1976. The Bank rate was rapidly lowered, falling to $7\frac{1}{2}$ per cent by May 1977. Output growth recovered by the end of the year, and the deterioration in unemployment began to stabilise by the first quarter of 1978.

c) *1978.* Though monetary growth had recovered somewhat, it again slowed sharply in early 1978. Moreover, unemployment showed little sign of improving further from its $8\frac{1}{2}$ per cent rate. In addition, non-food consumer price inflation seemed to have improved markedly. The Bank of Canada was, therefore, inclined to maintain a somewhat relaxed stance, but the long slide in Canadian dollar exchange rate that had characterized the entire period of relatively expansive monetary policy, and had been substantially exaggerated by political factors, finally came to be seen as an intolerable future inflation threat. Consequently, the monetary authorities began to orient Canadian credit conditions to those in the U.S. again for the first time in over two years. Following U.S. interest rate developments, the Bank of Canada raised its Bank rate seven times over the course of 1978, from $7\frac{1}{2}$ to $10\frac{3}{4}$ percent, primarily to protect the Canadian dollar. Assisted by a strong export performance, however, Canadian real economic activity held steady. Despite the authorities' moves, the Canadian dollar continued to depreciate through most of 1978. Along with surging food prices, this contributed to an acceleration of consumer price inflation during the year, reflected in a pickup of monetary growth. Nevertheless, the Bank of Canada reaffirmed its monetary "gradualism" policy by again shifting the M1 range lower in October 1978. The authorities apparently saw the recently recorded inflation rates as

Chart 9. MONETARY MANAGEMENT AND INTEREST RATE TRENDS: CANADA

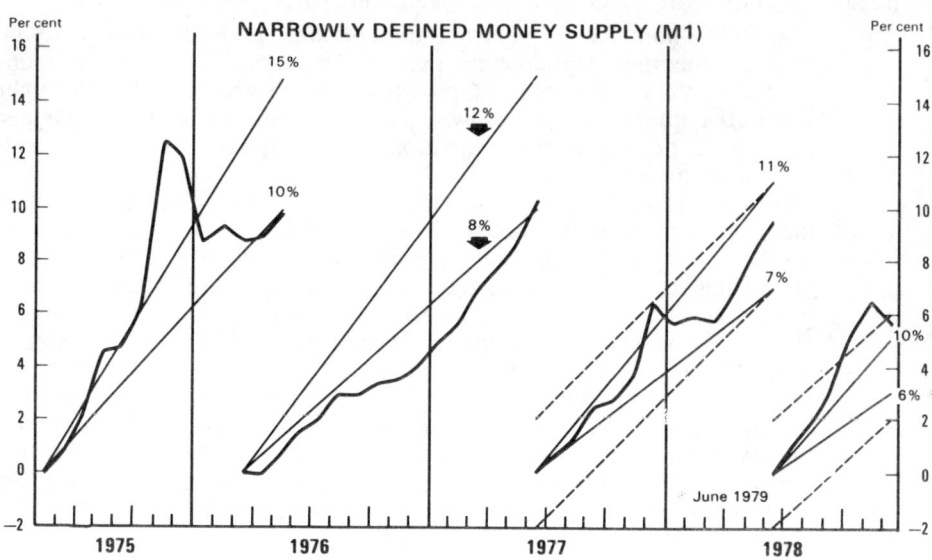

unrepresentative of the price inflation picture as reflected, for example, in continued moderate wage settlements. With increasing stability of the Canadian dollar, some moderation of exceptional food price rises, and labour markets still oversupplied, it was felt that price performance would improve substantially and that wage earners would avoid attempts to recoup real income losses, so that monetary objectives could be realized without undue strain.

Note to Charts 4, 5, 6, 7 and 9:

Targets or target ranges for the money supply shown for the *United States, France,* the *United Kingdom* and *Canada* are expressed as growth rates over four quarters or twelve month periods. Straight lines represent hypothetical "nominal" target paths or tolerance ranges which are compared with actual developments in target variables calculated as percentage changes of seasonally adjusted figures relative to the base quarter or month. For Canada, the target range for June 1977-June 1978 is viewed as a band of uniform width, the limits being 2 per cent above and below the mid point of the range.

For *Germany,* the target for the central bank money stock is expressed as a growth rate over twelve months during 1975 and as an annual average growth rate in subsequent years. Projected and actual developments shown for 1975 are plotted according to the same method as described above. For subsequent years, percentage changes are shown for the projected and actual cumulative monthly averages of the current year's central bank money stock against the twelve month average of the previous year.

Short-term interest rates shown in the middle or lower panels largely reflect the authorities' short-run operating strategy in the money market which—together with quantitative restrictions on bank credit in the case of France and the United Kingdom—is geared towards the achievement of the intermediate monetary target and ultimate policy goals. Policy-induced changes in short-term rates can normally be expected to exert a lagged influence on actual monetary growth and long-term market interest rates.

Money supply and interest rate series have been extracted from OECD and central bank publications. Money stock data for the United Kingdom do not take account of most recent revisions in seasonal adjustments.

III
BENEFIT AND COST OF MONETARY TARGETING

The overall achievements of target-oriented monetary management since the 1974-1975 recession and inflation bulge are extremely difficult to judge. Unusual uncertainties and disturbances characterised the mid-1970s. And a complex interaction of policy factors, "supply shock" absorption, and abnormally pronounced cyclical swings in general sentiment, price expectations and private spending have determined economic conditions in the recent period. The specific trends can hardly be disentangled with any degree of confidence or precision. Nevertheless, some tentative suggestions may be offered in order to facilitate a forward-looking evaluation of the potential cost and benefit of target-constrained monetary policies.

A. MONETARY PERFORMANCE

The materials presented in the Country Charts (Annex I) and Tables 3 (Introduction) and A (Annexe II) clearly indicate that monetary growth in most countries considered has been comparatively moderate since 1974-1975. Growth of "nominal" money stocks (M1 and M2/M3) has been distinctly lower than during the period of excessive monetary expansion in the early 1970s, notwithstanding expansionary monetary developments in *Germany* and *Switzerland* during 1978. This tendency towards medium-term deceleration is even more striking if the behaviour of "real" money balances is compared during the two periods. Weak output trends and embedded high cost inflation help account for this moderation, but it can also be partly attributed to conscious, if cautious, control by the authorities of key monetary aggregates and to circumspect fiscal policies.

Monetary management again appears to have been fairly successful, if the evolution of monetary authorities' preferred quantitative control variables (Table 3) is considered as a standard. In the *United States, France,* the *United Kingdom* and *Canada,* the authorities saw themselves in a position to bring down projected monetary growth rates or tolerance ranges gradually, following the first public announcement of monetary objectives. In *Germany,* official targets have remained steady; the Bundesbank published 8 per cent year-on-year or annual average growth targets for the central bank money stock each year from 1975 to 1978. Although substantial deviations occurred within projection periods, actual rates of monetary growth were rather close to target over twelve-month projection periods in most countries until 1977. Apart from *Germany,* where continuous "overshooting" from 1975 through 1978 has led to a cumulative statistical "overhang" in monetary growth, periods of "undershooting" and "overshooting" tended to be offsetting over the medium-run. In the *United States*, M1 growth moved more clearly out of tolerance ranges set 12 months before beginning in the second half of 1977, but by the end of 1978 was moving back into its range.

Year-on-year growth of broadly defined money in *Japan*, for which projections are now communicated to the public, has been nearly stabilised at a narrow 10-12 per cent range since early 1976. Quarterly "window guidance" of bank lending and unusually weak corporate demand for bank credit apparently enabled the authorities to direct monetary growth rather smoothly towards a desired medium-term path. At the same time, policy-controlled interest rates were adjusted downwards to historically low levels. In *Italy,* apart from the twelve-months period April 1974-March 1975, when actual values remained below target, total domestic credit expansion grew significantly faster in recent years than stipulated under official credit ceilings. As indicated in Chart 8 (Part II), heavy borrowing by the Treasury especially from domestic commercial banks and other financial institutions, which provided the financing for unexpectedly large budget deficits, and uncertainties as to the length of monetary impact lags, made financial control difficult.

B. INFLATION CONTROL AND EXTERNAL EQUILIBRIUM

The marked deceleration of inflation in most major countries, the calming of effective exchange rate movements in the *United Kingdom* and *Italy* after the 1976 exchange crises, and significant strengthening of current balances in several economies (Table 10) can to a considerable extent be viewed as a direct outcome of the medium-term strategy of cautious monetary restraint pursued since the mid-1970s. The stabilising of the effective dollar rate, after the tightening of monetary conditions by the Federal Reserve in November 1978, may be regarded as the most recent case in point, since this move appeared to signal the authorities' firm determination to moderate monetary growth and domestic inflation.

The effectiveness of target-constrained monetary management for controlling inflation cannot, of course, be read unambiguously from a simple examination of money and price movements over time, even when systematic allowance is made for lagged policy effects. Monetary stabilisation efforts have leaned conspicuously against uncertain inflationary expectations, a climate of despondency as to the controllability of accelerating wage/price spirals after the 1974 oil-price shock, and the distrust of the viability of weaker currencies in exchange markets. But a number of other forces have played important initiating or supplementary roles. In some countries—notably *Canada* and the *United Kingdom*—price and incomes policies seem to have been helpful, while others have benefited from restrictive or cautious budgetary policies or from exchange rate appreciation. Thus, while the general decline in inflation in the two to three years after 1974 can no doubt be associated in part with the pursuit of less accommodative medium-term monetary strategies, a balanced judgement on the contribution of monetary policies in themselves must also allow for these factors.

To a considerable extent the initiating or accommodative effect of monetary growth on inflation probably operates through the classic channels of variation in wealth and in rates of return on financial and real assets, in ways that can be captured in conventional econometric analysis. These basic macroeconomic relationships would probably be regarded by most economists as important for explaining the recent pattern of inflationary pressures and their control whereas

	1974			1975			1976			1977			1978		
	Projected 1	Actual 2	Diff. 2-1	Projected 1	Actual 2	Diff. 2-1	Projected 1	Actual 2	Diff. 2-1	Projected 1	Actual 2	Diff. 2-1	Projected 1	Actual 2	Diff. 2-1
United States															
Real GNP	2.5	—1.4	—3.9	—1.5	—1.3	0.2	7.0	6.0	—1.0	5.0	4.9	—0.1	4½-5	4.0	—0.7
Unemployment (%)		5.6		8.0	8.5	0.5	7.5	7.7	0.2	7.0	7.0	0	6-6½	6.0	—
Current Account (Bill. $)	5.0	—3.6	—8.6	—8.0	11.6	19.6	1.0	—1.4	—2.4	—1.0	—20.2	—19.2	—19¼	—16.0	3.2
Consumer Price Index	6.5	11.0	4.5	11.0	9.1	—1.9	6.2	5.8	—0.4	5.5	6.8	1.3	5¾-6¼	9.0	3.0
Effective Exchange Rate		—1.6			4.7			0.8			—5.1			—8.4	
M1 (Dec./Dec.)		5.1			4.1		4½-7½	5.8	—0.2	4½-6½	7.8	2.3	4-6½	6.7	1.5
Japan (Fiscal Year: March/March)															
Real GNP	2.5	—0.2	—2.7	4.3	3.4	—0.9	5.6	5.7	0.1	6.7	5.4	—1.3	7.0	5.5	—1.5
Unemployment (%)	1.3	1.5	0.2	1.4	2.0	0.6	1.7	2.0	0.3	1.9	2.1	0.2	2.0	2.2	0.2
Current Account (Bill. $)	—0.5	—2.3	—1.8	—1.7	0.1	1.8	—2.7	4.7	7.4	—0.7	14.0	14.7	6.0	12.0	6.0
Consumer Price Index	9.6	22.0	12.4	11.8	10.2	—1.6	8.8	9.4	0.6	8.4	6.7	—1.7	6.8	3.8	—3.0
Effective Exchange Rate		—6.2			2.6			8.3			15.3			8.3	
M2		11.3			15.4			12.8			10.5		12.0	12.6	0.6
Germany															
Real GNP	0-2	0.5	—0.5	2.0	—1.9	—3.9	4-5	5.1	0.6	5.0	2.6	—2.4	3.5	3.4	—0.1
Unemployment (%)	2.0	2.6	0.6	3.0	4.7	1.7	4½	4.6	0.1	4.0	4.5	0.5	4.5	4.3	—0.2
Current Account (Bill. $)	1.0	9.7	8.7	6.0	3.8	—2.2	2.0	3.8	1.8	5.0	3.8	—1.2	3.0	8.1	5.1
Consumer Price Index	8-9	7.0	—1.5	6.0	6.0	0	5-4½	4.5	—0.2	4.0	3.9	—0.1	3.5	2.6	—0.9
Effective Exchange Rate		3.9			—2.8			11.3			5.8			3.1	
Central Bank Money (annual average)		6.2		7¼	7.8	0.6	8.0	9.2	1.2	8.0	9.1	1.1	8.0	11.4	3.4
France															
Real GDP	5.0	2.8	—2.2	3.7	0.3	—3.4	4.5	4.6	0.1	4.6	3.3	—1.3	4.3	3.2	—1.1
Unemployment (%)	..	2.3		3.5	4.0	0.5	5.1	4.4	—0.7	4.7	5.0	0.3	6	5.6	—0.4
Current Account (Bill. $)	—0.8	—6.0	—5.2	—6.3	—0.1	6.2	—2.5	—6.1	—3.6	—3.8	—3.2	0.6	—2	3.2	5.2
Consumer Price Index	7.3	13.7	6.5	10.0	11.7	1.7	8.2	9.6	1.4	8.0	9.5	1.5	7.6	9.3	1.7
Effective Exchange Rate		—3.1			7.1			—12.4			—2.8			—1.1	
M2 (Dec./Dec.)		16.6			17.7			14.0		12.5	13.9	0.4	12	12.3	0.3
United Kingdom															
Real GDP	4.0	0.3	—3.7	1.8	—1.6	—3.4	2.4	2.1	—0.3	2.5	0.7	—1.8	2.0	3.0	1.0
Unemployment (%)	..	2.5		4.0	3.8	—0.2	5.7	5.3	—0.4	5.7	5.7	0	5.8	5.7	—0.1
Current Account (Bill. $)	—3.0	—8.1	—5.1	—6.5	—3.7	2.8	—3.2	—2.0	1.2	—3.3	—0.1	3.2	3.5	0.5	—3.0
Consumer Price Index	7.0	16.0	9.0	18.0	24.2	6.2	12.6	15.1	2.5	13.5	14.0	0.5	8.3	8.6	0.3
Effective Exchange Rate		—2.8			—9.3			—17.4			5.8			—2.7	
Sterling M3 (April/April)							9-13	7.8	—3.2	9-13	14.9	3.9	8-12	11.4	1.4
Italy															
Real GDP	6.0	4.2	2.2	0	—3.5	—3 5	2.0	5.7	3.7	0	1.7	1.7	2.0	2.4	0.4
Unemployment (%)	..	2.9		..	3.3		..	3.7		..	7.1			7.2	
Current Account (Bill. lire)	—700	—5 212	—4 512	—3 300	—377	2 923	—200	—2 343	2 143	500[a]	1 200[a]	700	1 800	5 400	3 600
Consumer Price Index	8	19.1	11.1	19.0	17.0	—2.0	10.0	16.7	6.7	19.0	18.4	—0.6	11.5	12.4	0.9
Effective Exchange Rate		—13.0			1.2			—22.6			—7.6			—7.0	
Domestic Credit (Dec./Dec.)	19.0[b]	16.5	—2.7	18.0[b]	22.4	4.6	17.8	19.8	2.0	16.0	17.8	1.8	19.3	21.2	1.9
Canada															
Real GNP	5½	3.6	—1.9	3.0	1.3	—1.7	5.3	5.5	0.2	3.7	2.7	—1.0	5.0	3.4	—1.6
Unemployment (%)		5.5			6.9			7.1			8.1			8.4	
Current Account (Bill. $)	—0.4	—1.5	—1.1	—1.5	—4.7	—3.2	—3.2	—4.2	—1.0	—3¼	—4.0	—¾	—3.75	—4.6	—0.9
Consumer Price Index		10.9		9½	10.8	1.3	9.0	7.5	—1.5	6.9	8.0	1.1	6.1	9.0	3.1
Effective Exchange Rate		0.3			—0.1			0			—11.1			—12.5	
M1[c]		15.4		10-15	10.0	—2.5	8-12	6.5	—3.5	7-11	8.5	—0.5	6-10	..	..

a) 12 months ending March (consistent with IMF target). *b)* Partly estimated from flows data. *c)* Twelve months beginning January 1974, May 1975, March 1976, June 1977 and 1978.

Sources: Projected data: Available national forecasts or projections at end of preceding calendar or fiscal year, or OECD Secretariat forecasts from December Economic Outlook. *Actual data:* OECD (except for Japan).

sociological or "structural" hypotheses[1] alone would be insufficient. On the other hand, the complexity and occasional instability of the estimated functions, notably the importance of interest rates, inflation and institutional changes in influencing the underlying money/income relationships, suggests that the causal linkages between the rate of monetary expansion and the rate of inflation are less direct and more complicated than is often claimed by "monetarist" economists. These problems invite continued research on the determinants of money velocity and increased attention to the development and evaluation of large-scale "structural" econometric models capable of capturing the special circumstances such as those characterising the recent period.

Perhaps the most important auxiliary channel through which monetary objectives policies may directly reduce inflation pressures is the announcement effect on public inflationary expectations. Communicating anti-inflationary policy intentions through publicly announced monetary objectives is a potentially powerful mechanism that appears to have been one rationale for the transition to targeting in several countries, notably in *Germany, Switzerland, France,* the *United Kingdom, Canada* and the *United States.* The absence of well-developed and empirically applicable models of the formation of expectations underlines the conjectural and experimental nature of the announcement effects of monetary targeting. While recent experience does suggest a potentially important linkage through the exchange rate, stabilising announcement effects on domestic price and wage behaviour are less obvious. Correct anticipation of the authorities' policy intentions by the public may serve to mitigate aggressive pricing and wage-bargaining behaviour *ex ante,* especially where the authorities have had an opportunity—as in *Germany* from 1974 to 1976—to prove their determination to accept the output and employment consequences of non-accommodative policy behaviour. On the other hand, a lack of public confidence in the technical or political feasibility of continued monetary targeting—as some observers have sometimes noted in the *United Kingdom*—could force the authorities into a situation in which the desired impacts on domestic expectations might at best be expected *ex post,* i.e. only after unusual real output losses have been incurred. In either case, attempts by the public to anticipate the inflationary consequences of monetary policy render all of the conventional guides of policy formulation difficult to interpret; and the authorities may well have chosen simply to publish monetary targets as a guide to financial markets.

C. POLICY COORDINATION

Package deals

An essential element in the formulation of a monetary target is the development of coordinated packages of non-inflationary government policies of which the target is one component. In *Germany, France,* and the *United Kingdom,* the derivation and announcement of monetary targets has been formally associated with government economic projections, budgetary programmes, and statements of government intention with respect to wage and price decisions. A tightening of monetary conditions in November 1978 was a constituent of a similar anti-inflationary policy approach in the *United States.* Such procedures are especially useful in the context of the limited ability of economic agents to translate monetary targets directly into macroeconomic implications for

---

1. Such hypotheses typically attribute inflation to wage pressures resulting from bargaining procedures, administrative pricing decisions, supply bottlenecks and related microeconomic phenomena.

prices and economic activity or to convert that information into appropriate microeconomic decisions. More broadly based policy packages should enhance the announcement effects of monetary targets and could ultimately serve to widen the scope for discretionary monetary management to the extent that firms and labour groups show increased self-restraint in price/wage determination, complying with official orientation data or global guidelines.

Budget financing

Monetary growth objectives linked to government borrowing needs can provide a valuable mutual consistency check and a signal of the coherence of official stabilisation policy. Large public-sector deficits that persisted during the period under review in several OECD economies called into question the compatibility of the increased borrowing requirements with target-constrained monetary policies. The most obvious conflict can arise through the classic "crowding-out" mechanism in which public borrowing drives up interest rates, reduces the value of private wealth and serves to replace rather than augment private economic activity. The quantitative importance of these offsets has proved difficult to measure, and their significance remains controversial. More immediately relevant in some countries may be the psychological and institutional obstacles to direct government borrowing: adverse announcement effects on market interest rates and private borrowing intentions, imperfections in capital markets, and lack of sufficient private demands for government bonds in countries with less well-developed securities markets (*Japan, France, Denmark*). The existence of such obstacles would point to a need for stronger monetary accommodation of employment-supporting fiscal action than might be deemed compatible with the requirement of moderate and steady medium-term monetary growth. Similarly complicating factors were apparent in the temporary financial instabilities that prevailed when large budget deficits arose during the past recession: business balance sheet consolidation, uneven sectoral distribution of private activity and related money and credit demands, unusual fluctuations in household saving ratios, and—in a few countries, including notably the *United States*—unpredicted movements in money demand relationships. Temporary increases in demand for money and distortion of money supply statistics associated with large tax cuts or direct tax rebates have, at times, also reduced the information content of short-run monetary aggregates movements.

Exchange rate constraints

Erratic and unpredicted disturbances in exchange markets have placed further constraints on the autonomous pursuit of national monetary targets and the coordination of government financial objectives. The most obvious example of the growing importance of external influences is the feedback from exchange-rate depreciation to domestic inflation in the *United States* and the associated impact on domestic liquidity from heavy dollar intervention in appreciating currency countries during 1977-1978 (*Japan, Germany, United Kingdom, Switzerland*). Similar feedback effects had been observed in countries temporarily exposed to crisis conditions (*Italy* in 1975-1976, *United Kingdom* in 1976) and in "dependent" economies either on floating rates (*Canada*), or linked to strong currencies (*Belgium, Denmark*). Faced with erratic fluctuations in exchange rates, the authorities in virtually all major countries have, at times, had to decide whether priority should be given to initial interest rate and monetary aggregate objectives or explicit management of the exchange rate. With the latter sometimes regarded as a competing intermediate target of overall monetary management, temporary departures from domestic monetary objectives have been tolerated—

with efficient control of disorderly exchange market conditions apparently being viewed as an acceptable "trade-off".

These external linkages, which have imposed constraints on both strong- and weak-currency countries when national monetary policies have been seen to be internationally inconsistent, do not necessarily mitigate the desirability of target-based monetary strategies. To some extent, they may reflect a need for more domestic monetary instruments to manage the liquidity effects of exchange market intervention. Perhaps more fundamentally, they suggest the usefulness of more careful exploration of alternative combinations of fiscal and monetary policies within each country, and, at the international level, the need and chance for better *ex ante* coordination of internal and external national monetary objectives, especially in the largest "dominant" economies.

D. OPPORTUNITY COSTS FOR OUTPUT AND EMPLOYMENT

As inflation expectations became more entrenched at fairly high levels in several economies in the latter part of the period under review, public opinion and policy makers became more concerned about the potential costs of independent "pure monetary" stabilisation. Some confidence in the existence of short-or long-run trade-offs between inflation and desired employment or activity levels seemed likely to return. A strategy of gradually reducing monetary growth in the face of stubborn, fully anticipated cost inflation was thus increasingly being viewed as rather costly.

There is probably not much disagreement that the results of the combination of fiscal and monetary policies adopted notably in the three largest economies after 1974-1975 were acceptable, at least for a while. The initial behaviour of policy-controlled short-term interest rates and of monetary aggregates would suggest a cautiously expansionary monetary policy after the onset of the 1974-1975 recession; and a strategy of relatively steady longer-run monetary growth generally prevailed during the subsequent hesitant recovery in 1976-1977. This allowed expansionary fiscal impulses initiated in 1975 and the cyclical turnaround in stockbuilding and personal saving to work themselves out smoothly, with long-term market interest rates declining or remaining fairly stable (Charts Annex I).[2] However, lack of vigour in the overall recovery and the weak response of business fixed investment led, especially in 1977 and early 1978, to growing concerns about the appropriateness of continued monetary and fiscal caution.

Towards the end of 1978, increasing attention was being paid to apparent failures of many governments to achieve real economic goals together with lower inflation and reduced monetary growth (Table 10). Large and persistent current surpluses had emerged in *Japan, Germany* and *Switzerland* against the background of considerable under-utilisation of resources and weak domestic demand growth. In *Canada* and *France,* stabilisation gains on the inflation front had been relatively modest, while output growth decelerated more significantly than expected. In the *United Kingdom,* real output grew very sluggishly throughout the period, employment never returned to its pre-1974-1975 level, and a continued reduction in inflation proved elusive. Moreover, the difficulty the British authorities had in ensuring—with the available policy instruments—a smooth path of

---

2. The behaviour of long-term interest rates may over-estimate the actual degree of monetary accommodation, since inflation premia probably had diminished over the medium-term due to decelerating inflationary expectations. Moreover, longer-term market interest rates in *Japan* were subject to administrative influence.

monetary growth, led to substantial variability of market interest rates which, at times, may have affected private spending decisions. In *Italy,* the recent strengthening of the current account and modest deceleration of inflation were achieved under the influence of overall monetary restraints, with high public sector deficits persisting. Treasury borrowing requirements have tended to depress private investment demand—and thus the economy's future growth and export potential—through the working of financial "crowding-out" mechanisms. The *United States* economy seemed to move quickly from a state of hesitant growth and resource under-utilisation to excess demand and a strong inflation surge. In most countries, reduced rates of price inflation and nominal wage increase have generally not served to bring "real" wage and profit relationships into balance, so as to permit a lasting recovery of investment in a non-inflationary environment, and "real" exchange rate changes sometimes proved costly to implement and difficult to sustain.

On the other hand, it could be argued that the moderate overall outcome of economic management to date was partly due to hesitant or overly flexible pursuit of "non-accommodating" policies. Wide swings in exchange rates and frictions in the real economy undoubtedly played an important role as well; supply problems at the micro-level, protectionism, economic inefficiencies, and structural adjustment problems associated with the new energy situation and increased competition from newly industrialised countries are notable examples of the latter.

CONCLUDING REMARKS

Although the transition to monetary targeting can be traced back to the 1960's, the actual policy experience is relatively short and it is difficult to draw very precise conclusions. Nevertheless, among those OECD countries which have adopted such policies, there seems to be a consensus on the following points:

a) with a roughly predictable or at least understandable relationship between money or credit and nominal GNP, persistent indications of growth of such aggregates above targets can be seen as a warning signal of rising inflation (or excess demand pressure). Thus, the monitoring of monetary aggregates can give valuable assistance in expediting a counter-cyclical monetary policy and, at a minimum, provide important information for formulation of policy;

b) although there is no uniform view on the underlying mechanism and though there is doubt as to the existence of any direct link between announcement of monetary targets and trade union and business attitudes, publicised money or credit aggregates objectives can be seen as increasing the efficiency of monetary policy by stabilising public expectations about inflation. In particular, if exchange markets react to a credible programme of monetary retrenchment and the currency stabilises or appreciates ahead of the actual improvement in domestic inflation, the adoption of limits to monetary growth may directly ease inflationary pressures through lower import price inflation;

c) more broadly, the setting of upper limits on monetary growth may be seen to communicate the authorities' willingness to subordinate short-term output objectives to the fight against inflation. By implying a point beyond which growth in nominal income will not be tolerated, monetary targets may reduce the risk of ever-higher inflation rates and, at a minimum, bound inflation uncertainties.

Money velocity is likely to be rather predictable over the medium term, but significantly less so in the short run. This uncertainty poses severe problems for the practical implementation of target-oriented monetary management, complicating and sometimes frustrating exploitation of the advantages cited above:

a) with velocity subject to erratic short-run movements, changes in monetary aggregates become a less reliable indicator, possibly delaying a propitious policy response or triggering an inappropriate policy reaction. Other economic indicators play a crucial role. The behaviour of monetary aggregates is only one source of information, and not necessarily the best. Indeed, there is still considerable uncertainty as to the extent to which the behaviour of the aggregates, especially over the shorter term, should dominate the stance of monetary policy;

b) with strict adherence to monetary targets in the short run at times carrying unacceptable costs, the consequent observed deviation between actual money growth and targets could limit stabilising announcement effects on inflationary expectations. Indeed, failure to achieve targets, even if only due to vagaries of the demand for money, might quickly check progress on the inflation front if the exchange markets reacted unfavourably.

More generally, the choice of a money or credit target variable may depend on the size of the country involved as well as the influence of external factors, and in a number of countries it may be difficult to reconcile external and internal goals. However, since this report is focused particularly on more traditional domestic linkages in those countries which have introduced monetary targets, these issues received little attention but may need to be more specifically addressed in a comprehensive assessment of monetary policy as a means to reducing inflation.

Annex I

COUNTRY CHARTS

CHART A1

GENERAL ECONOMIC INDICATORS
UNITED STATES

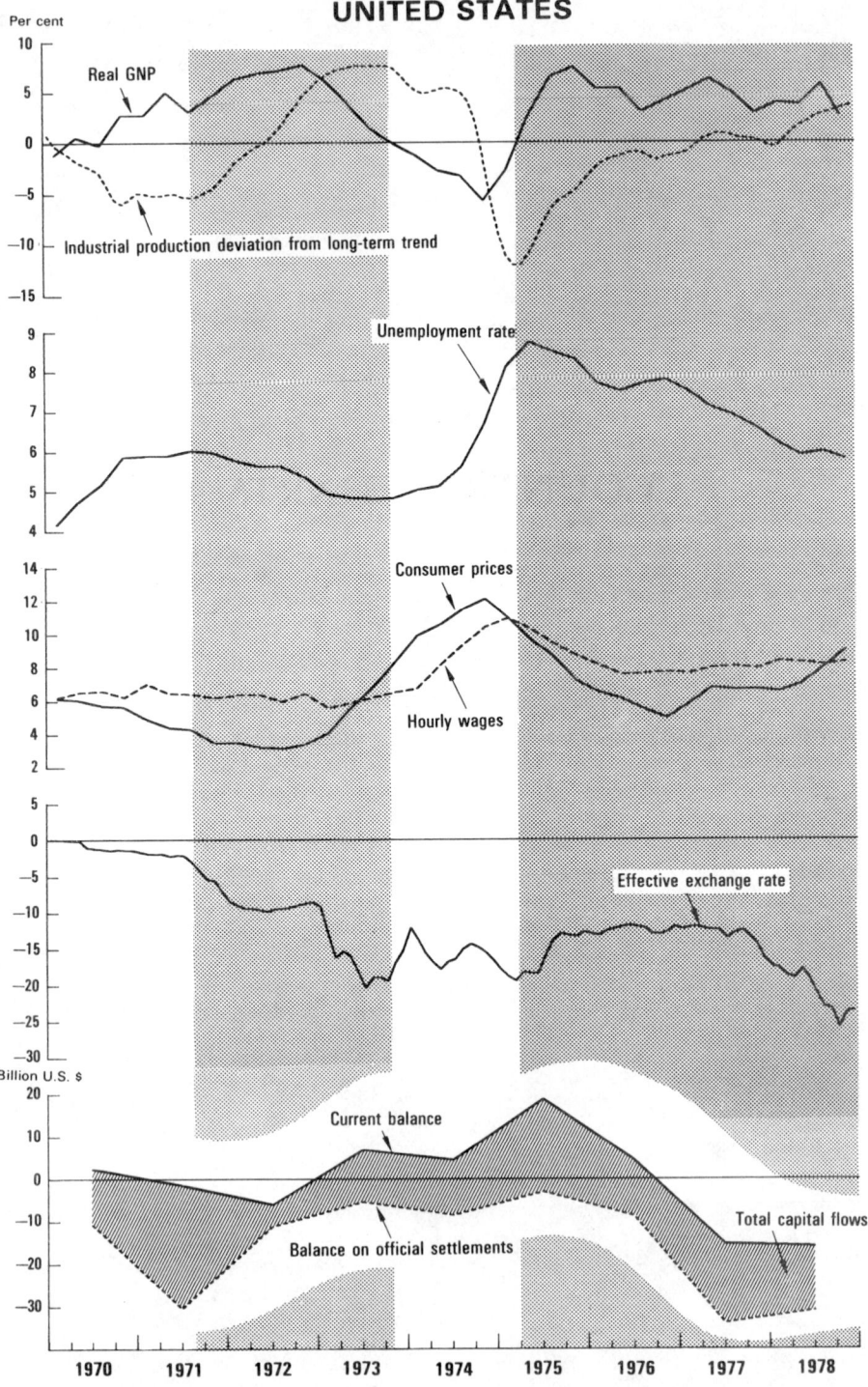

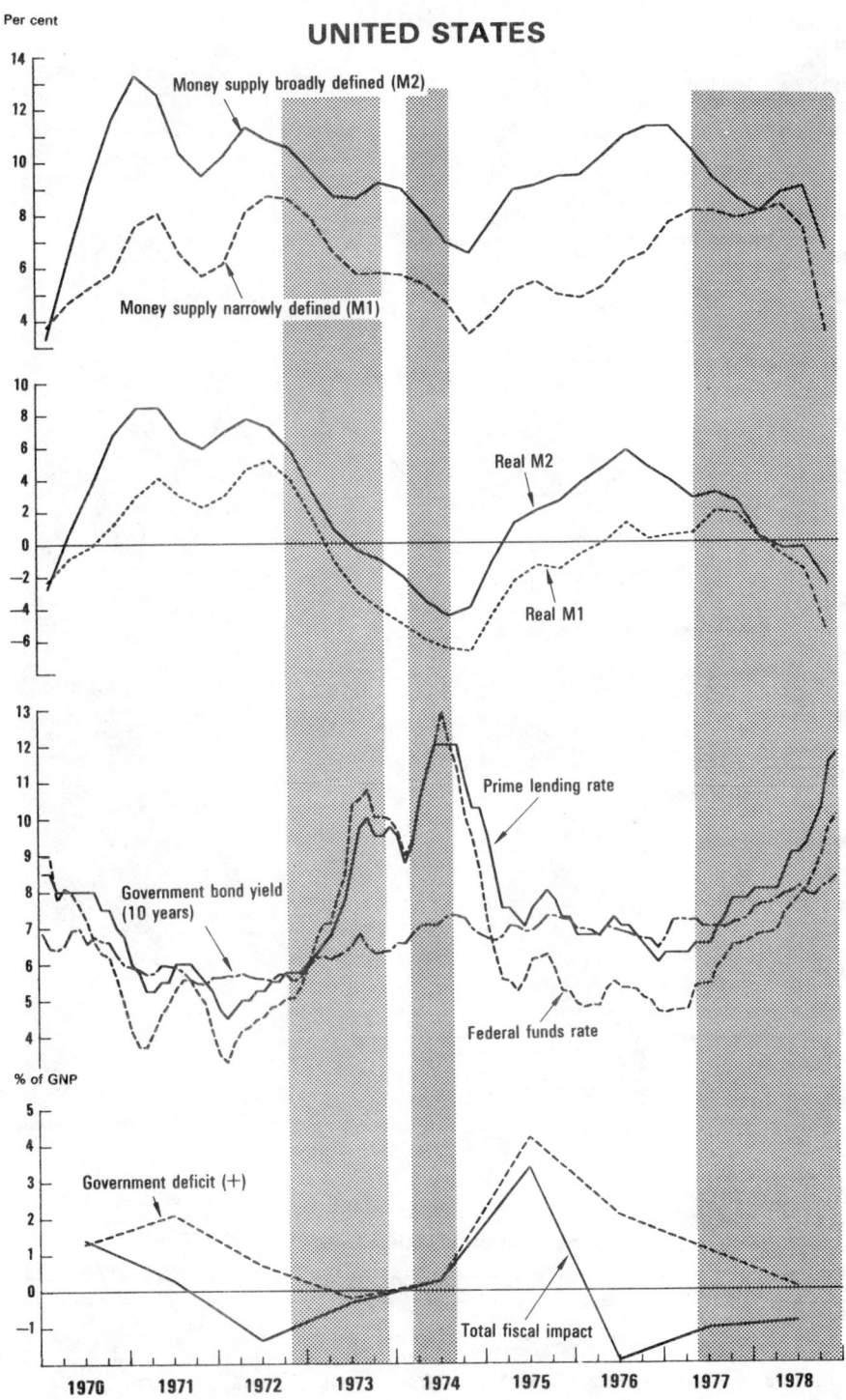

CHART B 1

POLICY INDICATORS
UNITED STATES

CHART A 2

GENERAL ECONOMIC INDICATORS
JAPAN

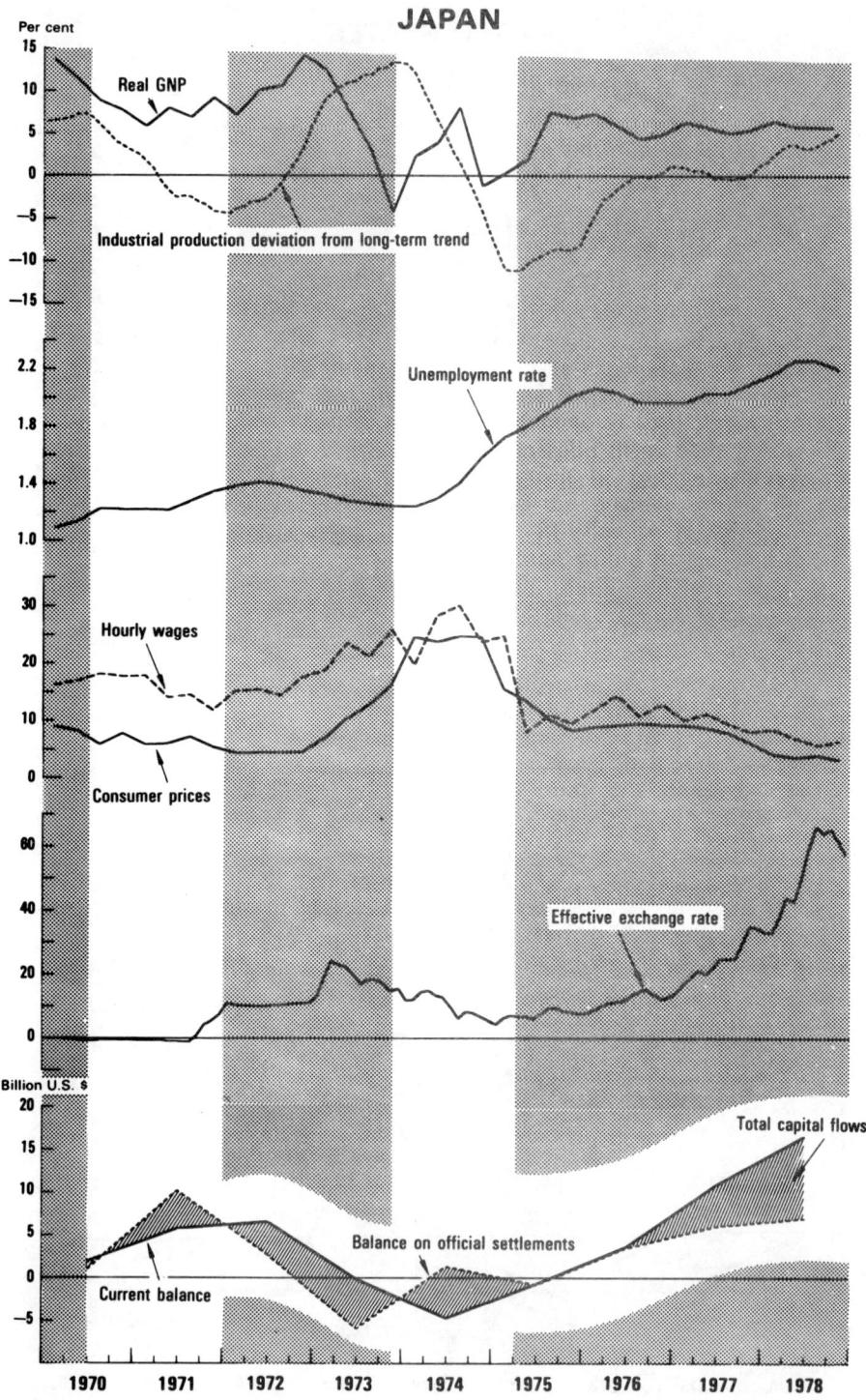

CHART B 2

POLICY INDICATORS
JAPAN

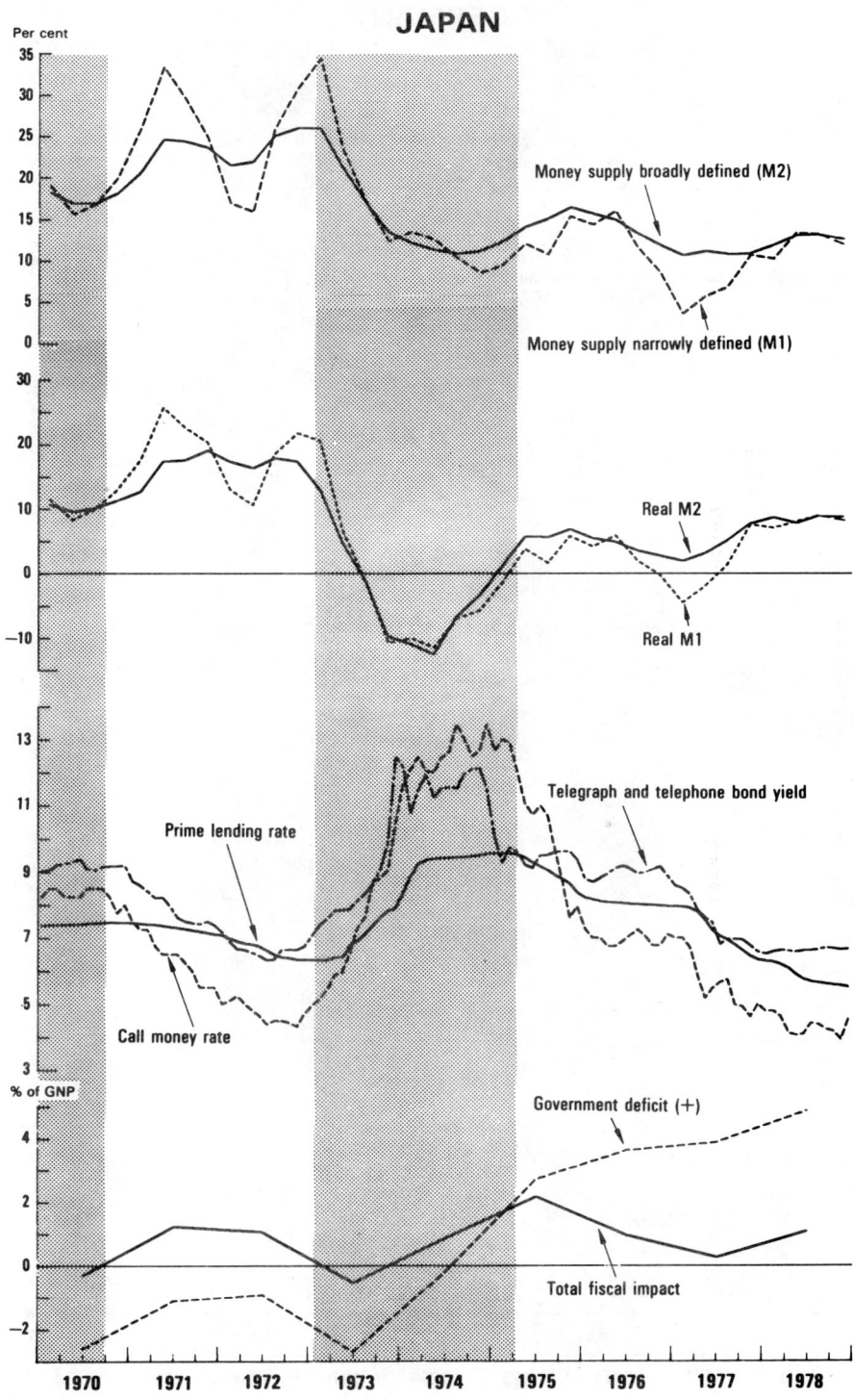

CHART A 3

GENERAL ECONOMIC INDICATORS
GERMANY

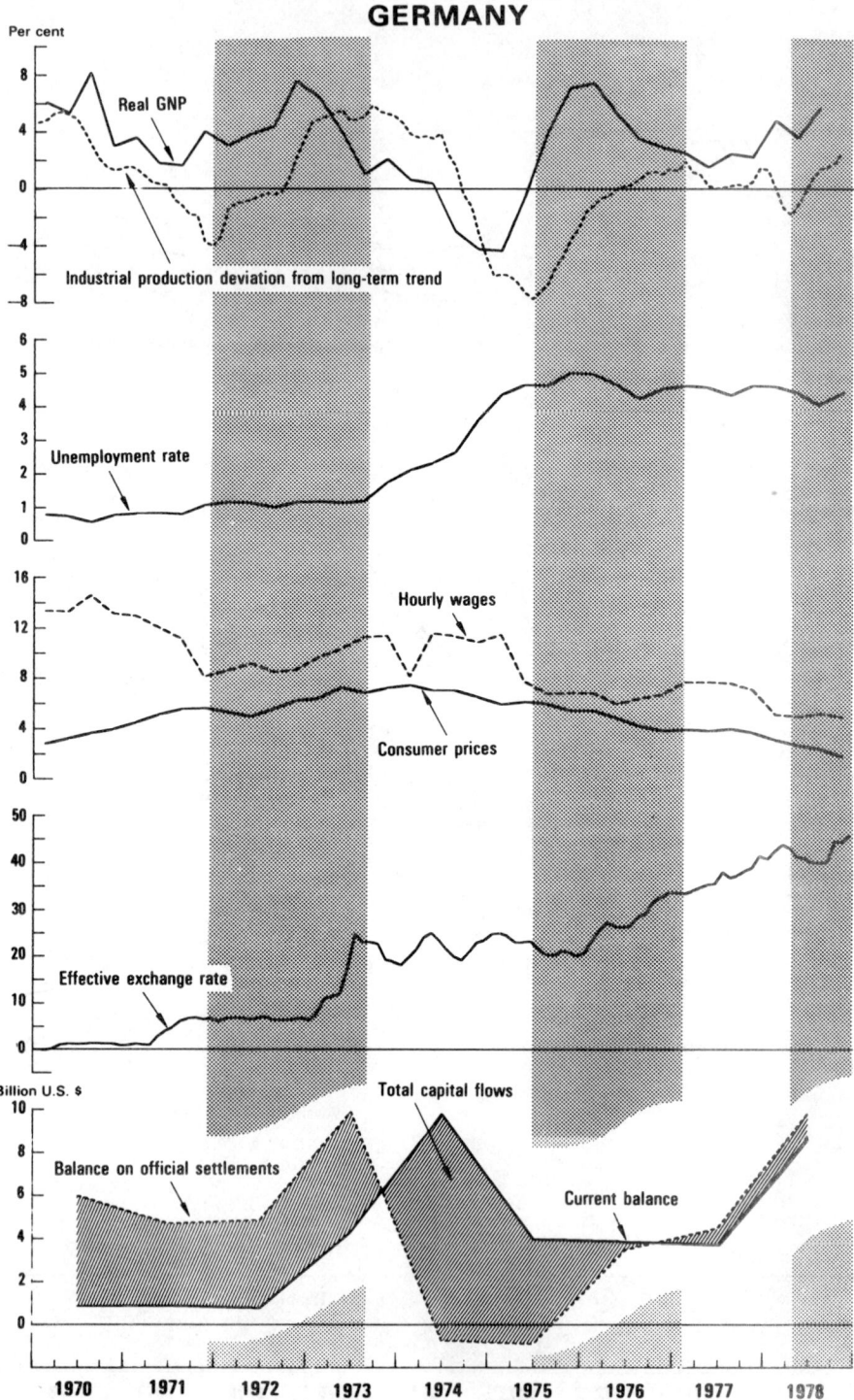

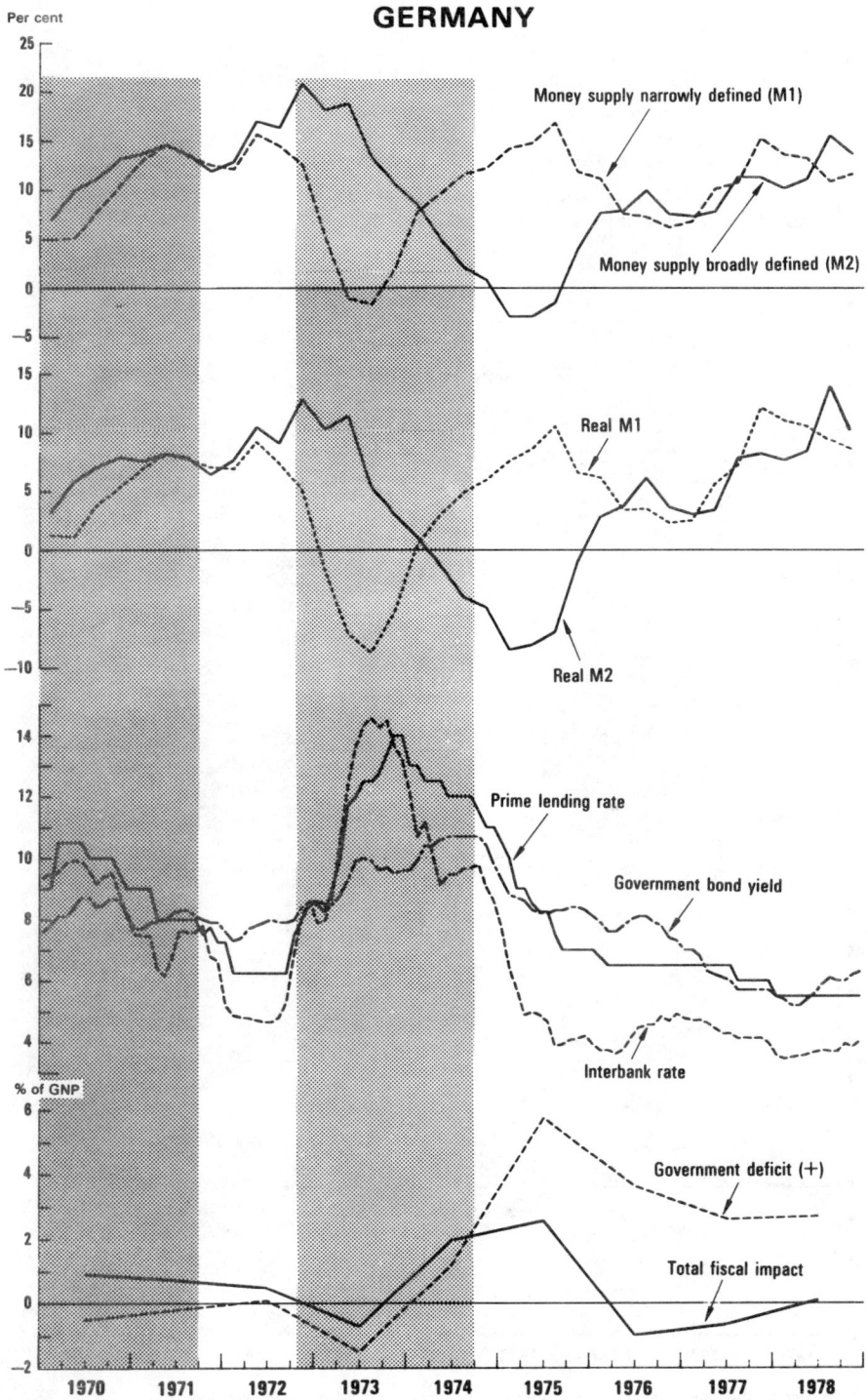

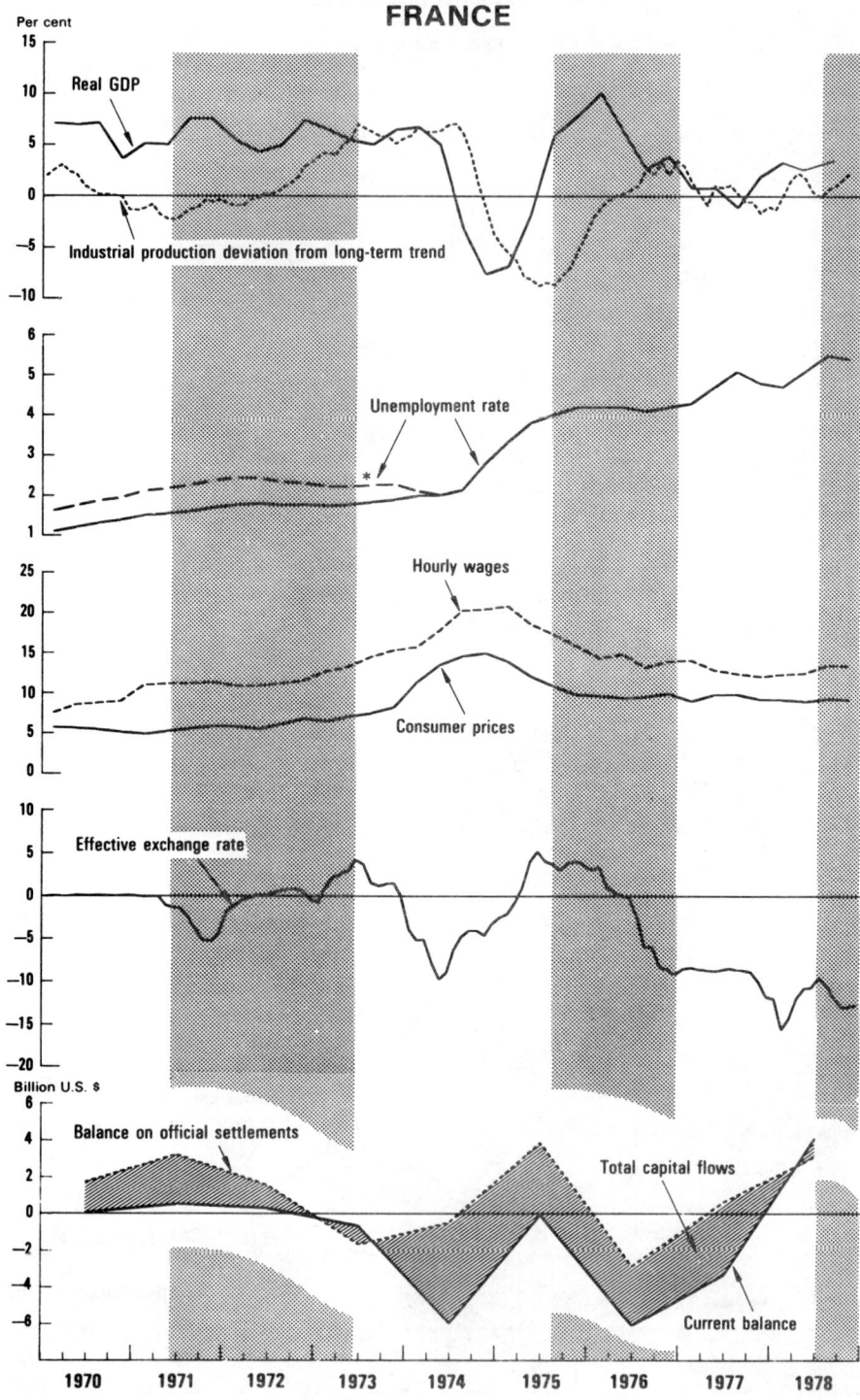

CHART A 4
**GENERAL ECONOMIC INDICATORS
FRANCE**

* Allowing for the repercussions of the progressive implementation of the *Agence Nationale pour l'Emploi*.

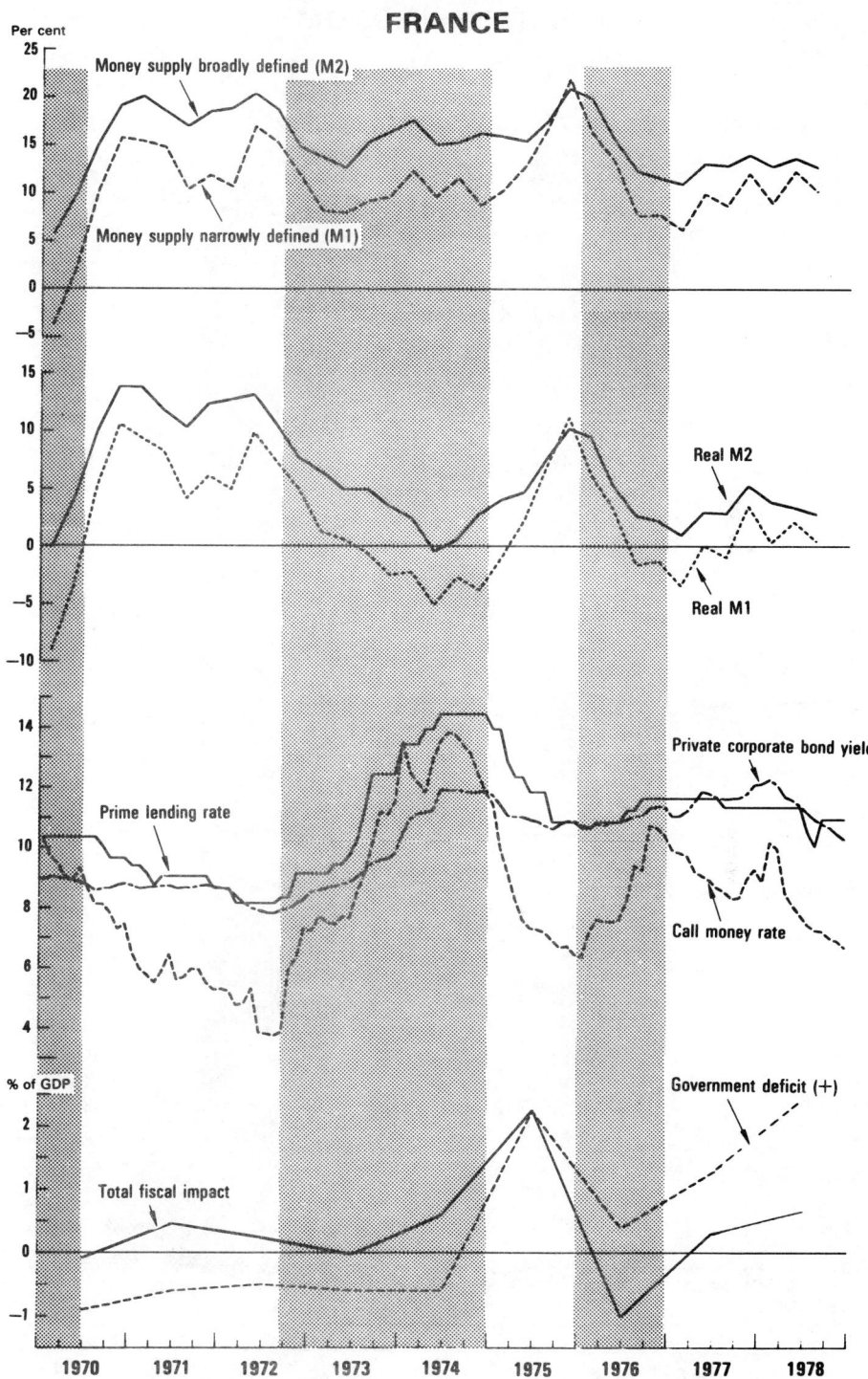

CHART A 5

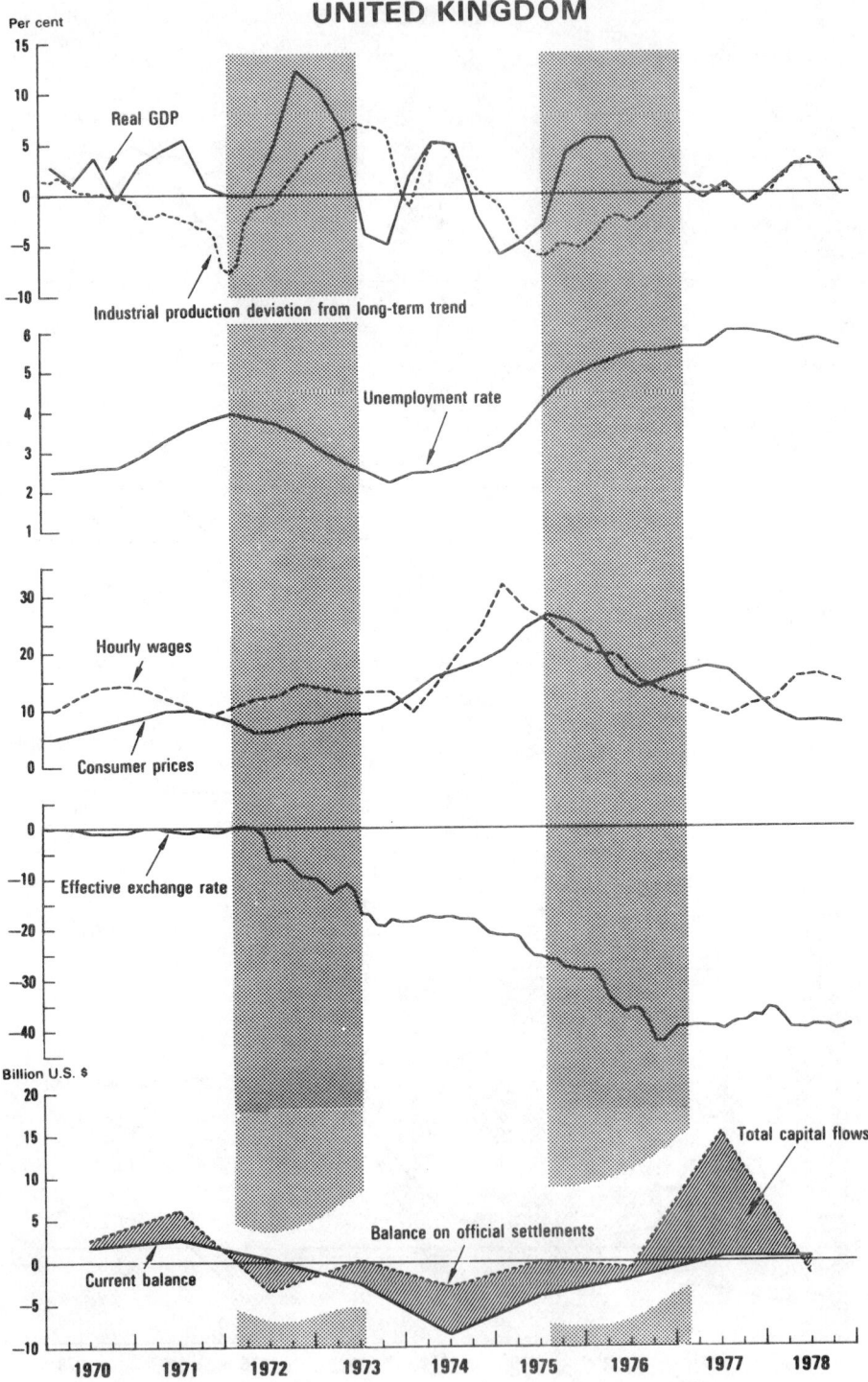

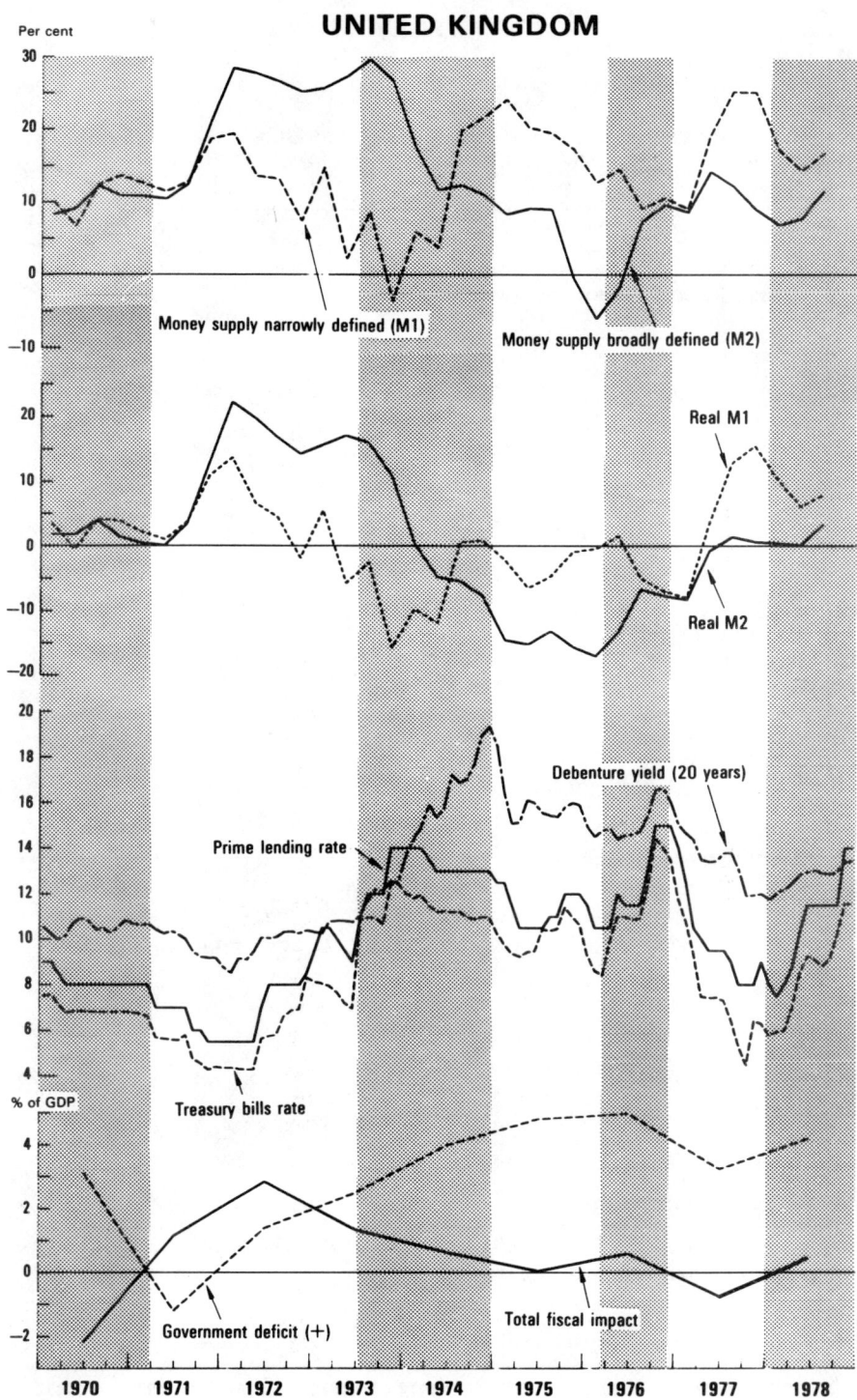

CHART B5

POLICY INDICATORS
UNITED KINGDOM

CHART A6

GENERAL ECONOMIC INDICATORS
ITALY

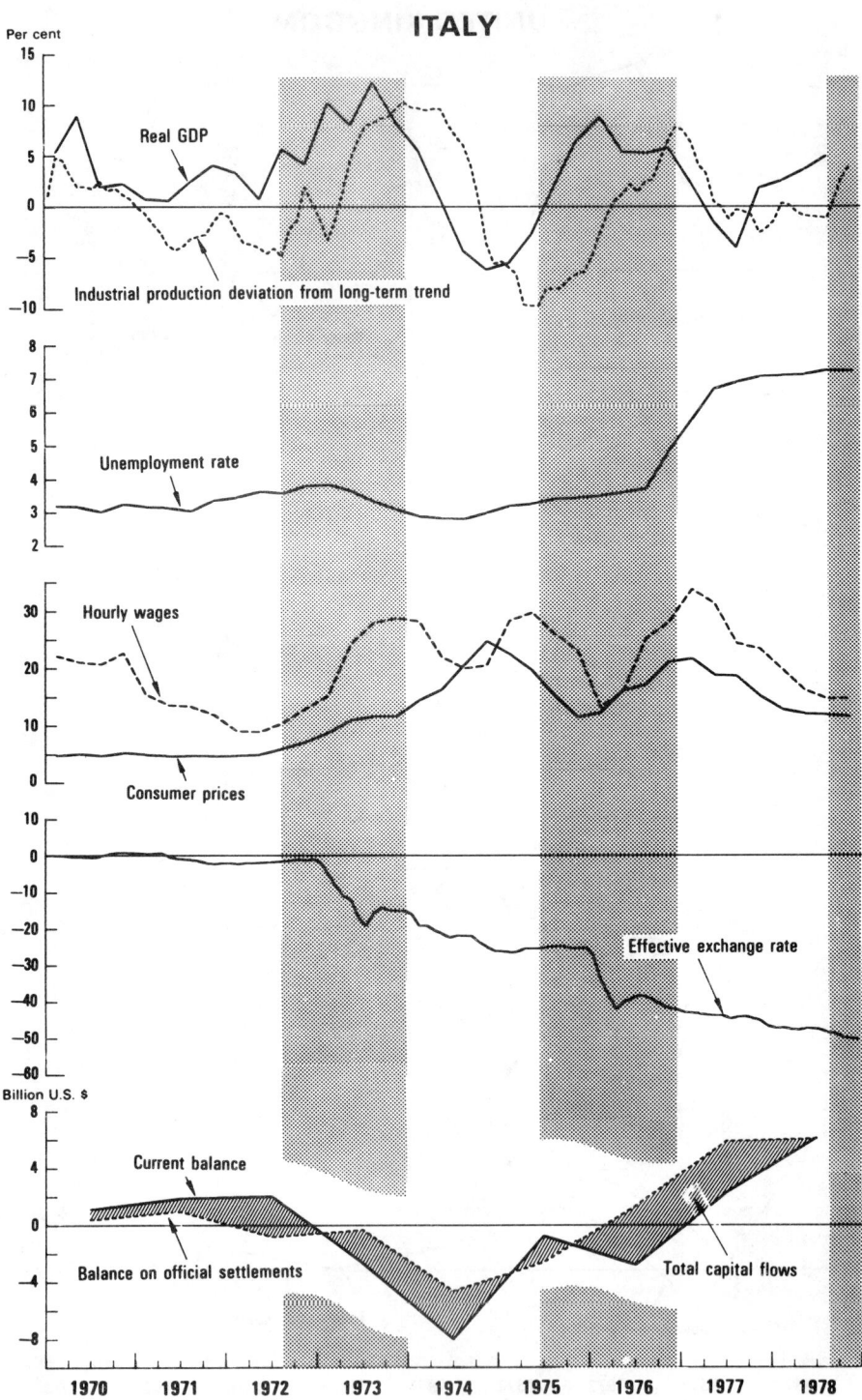

CHART B6

POLICY INDICATORS
ITALY

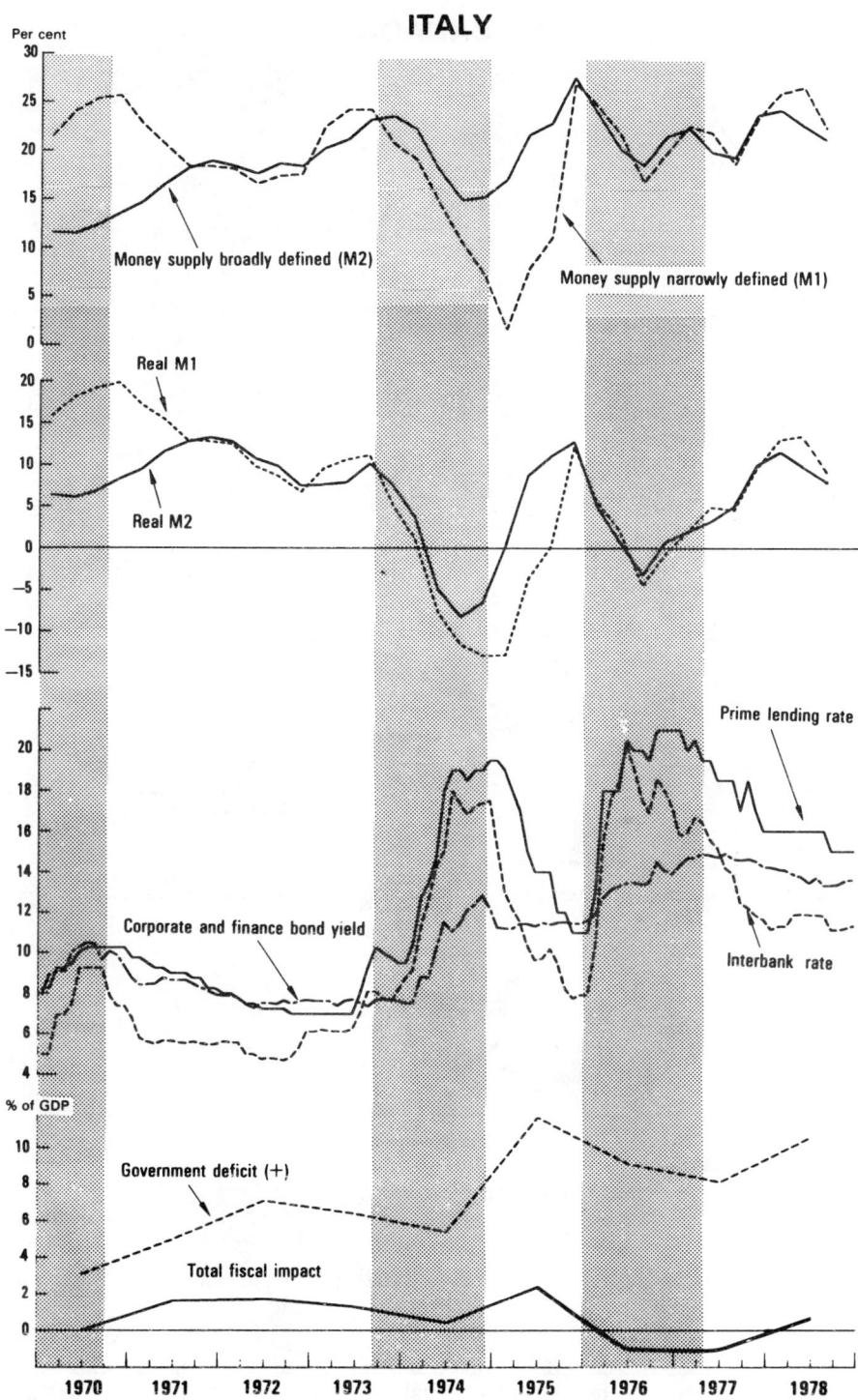

CHART A 7

GENERAL ECONOMIC INDICATORS
CANADA

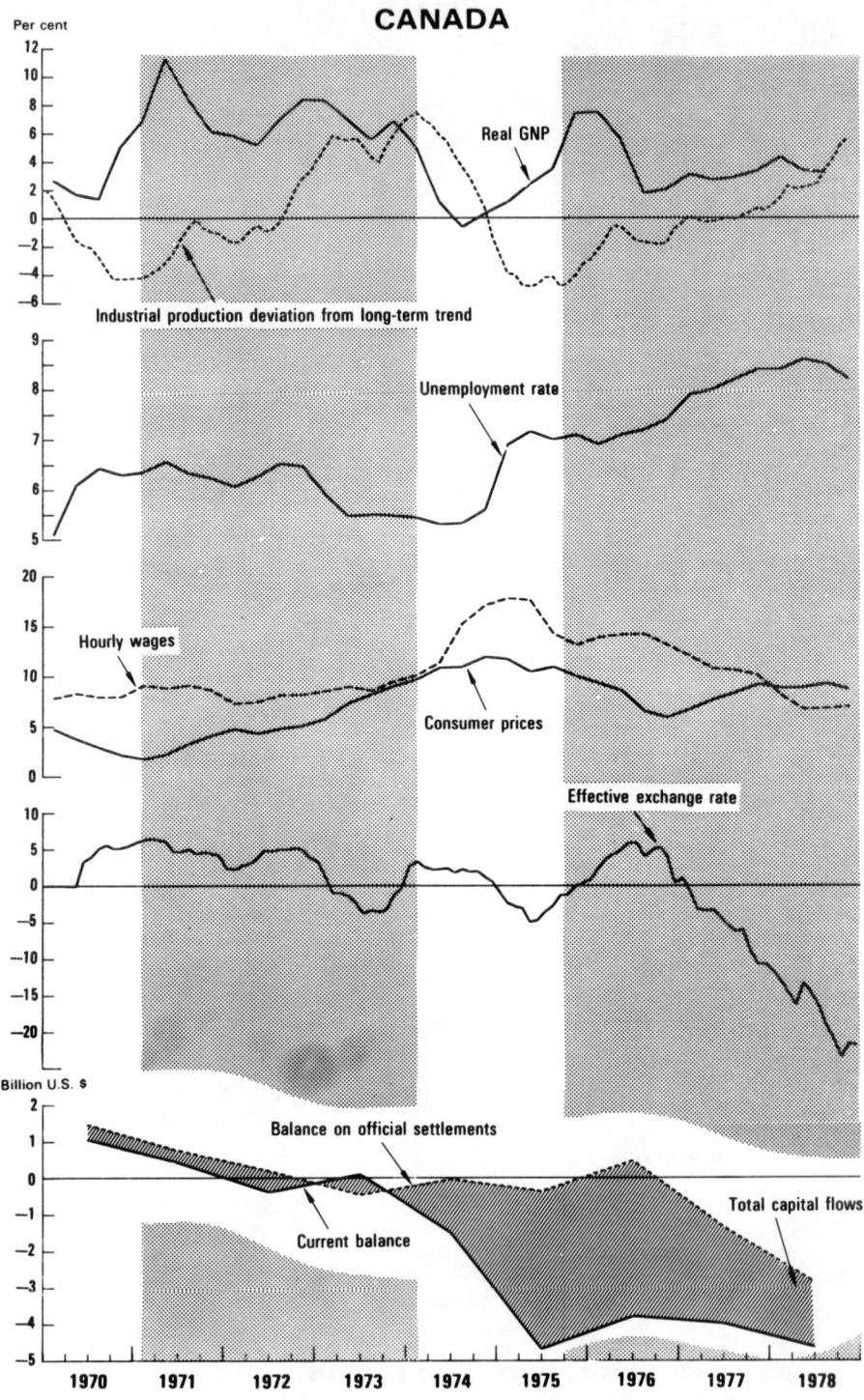

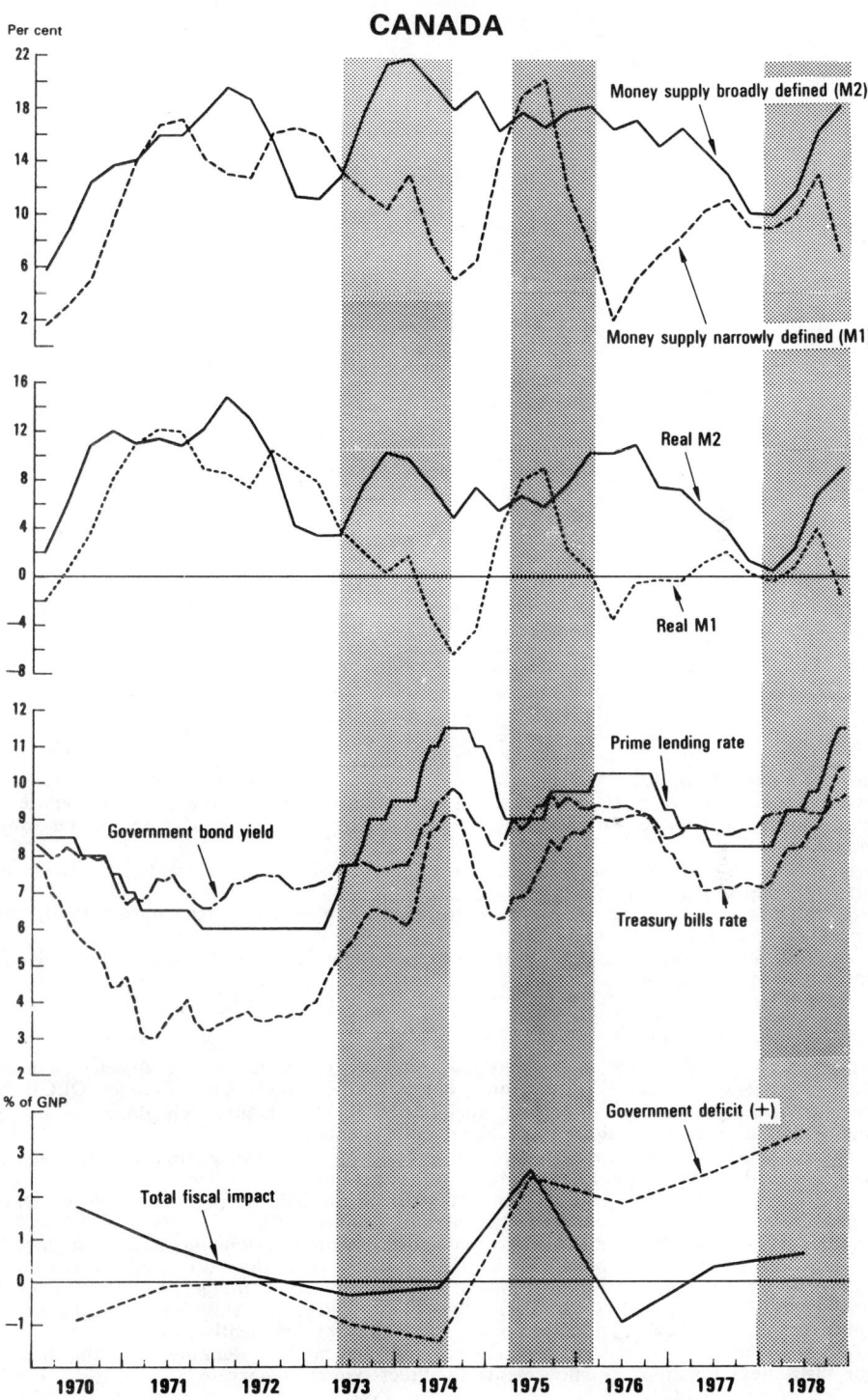
CHART B 7
POLICY INDICATORS
CANADA

Note to Charts A1 to A7.
Movements in *real GNP (GDP)* represent percentage changes over previous quarters at annual rates, calculated from seasonally adjusted data smoothed with three quarter moving averages.
Movements in *consumer prices* and *hourly wages* are shown as percentage changes over the corresponding quarter of the previous year.
Effective exchange rates are shown as percentage changes from 1st quarter 1970, based on weekly averages of daily figures.
Shaded areas indicate upswing periods of industrial production (troughs to peaks of deviations from long-term trend).
Source: OECD.

Note to Charts B1 to B7.
Movements in *money stock data* (seasonally adjusted) are shown as quarter-on-quarter percentage changes at annual rates (three quarter moving average). *Source:* OECD and various national publications. Money stock series for the United Kingdom do not take account of most recent revisions in seasonal adjustments.
"Real" M1 and M2 (M3) represents the growth of the money supply, narrowly and broadly defined, deflated by the consumer price increases.
Interest rates or yields are generally shown at, or near ends of periods. *Source:* OECD, Morgan Garanty Trust and various national publications.
Government deficits correspond to general government net lending according to SNA definitions. *Source:* OECD National Accounts. Total *fiscal impacts* have been estimated by the OECD Secretariat; for method of calculation, see "Budget Indicators", OECD Economic Outlook, Occasional Studies, July 1978. Figures for Italy do not take account of most recent revisions in national accounts which are not sufficiently extensive.
Shaded areas indicate restrictive periods of monetary policy delimited on the basis of major instrumental actions or movements in direct operating targets.

Annex II

THE EXPERIENCE OF SMALLER OPEN ECONOMIES

Socio-economic conditions in OECD countries outside the seven largest economies are not homogeneous enough to permit a summary assessment of their recent monetary experience. This section takes an eclectic approach reviewing central banking practices in three Northern European countries with sizeable manufacturing sectors and financial systems interacting with neighbouring countries. Exchange rate considerations consequently play a very important role in the conduct of monetary policies. The selection made, while necessarily somewhat arbitrary, is intended to represent different basic options in monetary policy approaches. The sample group encompasses one country practising a managed floating rate system (*Switzerland*), one operating "dual" exchange rates (*Belgium*), and one which has shown a comparatively strong preference for fixed but adjustable exchange rates (*Denmark*).

SWITZERLAND

The transition to a system of "managed floating" was accompanied by a new formulation of monetary policy aiming at consistent control of the money supply. Since the central bank no longer had to intervene systematically in the exchange market, it became possible to attempt to practise a more autonomous monetary policy. This prospect seemed attractive to the Swiss authorities notably with a view to ensuring price stability, which has been a matter of priority concern ever since the acceleration of world inflation. In 1975 the central bank began setting and publicly announcing a quantitative target for monetary expansion with the following main characteristics:

— the monetary aggregate—chosen as a target variable on the basis of empirical investigations—is the narrowly defined money supply M1;[1]
— the target is expressed in terms of a yearly average rate of growth, this rate being set in such a way as to make monetary expansion relatively stable over the medium term;
— the target is geared to the rate of growth envisaged for real GNP and the GNP deflator.

The target for maximum growth of M1 was set at 6 per cent for 1975 and 1976, and then reduced to 5 per cent for 1977 and 1978. On past experience and potential growth estimates for the Swiss economy, the monetary authorities consider that the monetary growth rate should be held at between 2 and 7 per cent over the medium term. This means that year-to-year average growth

---

1. Notes and coin in circulation and sight deposits of non-bank sector residents with the banks and in postal cheque accounts.

of M1 could vary within a relatively large margin. Moreover, Swiss monetary policy implicitly takes into account the importance of exchange rate fluctuations for a small economy heavily dependent on foreign trade. In intervening to avert extreme overshooting of Swiss franc exchange rate in relation to relative inflation performance, the authorities have shown themselves willing to accept M1 growth appreciably "off target". Indeed, in the face of mounting upwards speculation on the franc, the priority accorded to exchange rate stability increased through 1978, and led the authorities to announce late in the year their firm intention to tolerate no further appreciation of the franc against the deutschemark, regardless of the monetary consequences. This announcement was followed by the decision to temporarily suspend the setting of an explicit monetary objective for 1979. Thus, the Swiss authorities by no means adopt a rigid view to aggregates objectives; rather, these are seen as medium- to long-term constraints in a context of short-run flexibility, particularly in view of exchange rate disturbances.

As the money market is not well developed in Switzerland, adjustment of short-term interest rates is not sufficient to control monetary growth. Consequently, achievement of the growth target for M1 has depended more on direct control of the monetary base.[2] The latter, in a certain way, has served as a short-run operational target for monetary policy. In practice, the trend in the monetary base depends mainly on the changes in the official net foreign position, i.e. on the central bank's interventions in the exchange market. In order to "mop up" the liquidity changes resulting from external capital transactions, commercial banks have been required to convert into foreign exchange with the central bank the counterpart of loan issues by non-residents which are subject to authorisation.[3] In addition, the monetary authorities have had to tighten their controls on capital inflows when speculation on exchange rate appreciation intensified.[4] To a certain extent, the control of base money operates also through regulation of central bank credit to the banks in the form of discount facilities, advances against collateral and short-term dollar/franc swaps; in fact, given the importance of these swap transactions, central bank refinancing has become increasingly consonant with exchange rate considerations in recent years.

Chart C indicates that average growth of M1 was kept close to target in 1975 and 1977. On the other hand, an overshooting of two percentage points was recorded in 1976, which essentially reflected a shift from time deposits to sight deposits associated with lowering of interest rates on savings. In 1978, M1 growth was far above its target level for the year as a whole, resulting from massive official intervention on the exchange market to counteract a further appreciation of the franc. In fact, the overall outcome since 1975 has been achieved under abnormal external conditions. Under the fixed exchange rate system, the central bank had intervened less actively—albeit more systematically —on the exchange market, and the net increase in foreign exchange reserves during 1975-1978 was historically large if the exceptional experience of 1971 is disregarded.[5] Despite a continual decline in interest rates, the monetary

2. Defined as the sum of money in circulation and bank reserves.
3. Foreign loan issues on the capital market and credit to abroad.
4. Raising of the negative interest on non-residents deposits, increase in the banks' minimum reserve assets against foreign liabilities, restrictions on forward sales of Swiss francs, ban on purchases of Swiss securities, etc.
5. In 1975, the Swiss National Bank acquired foreign exchange equivalent to Swiss francs 11 billion and sold the equivalent of Swiss francs 9 billion to capital exporters. The figures were 18.8 and 15.5 billion respectively in 1976, 15.5 and 11.5 billion in 1977, and 22.5 and 12.1 billion in 1978.

CHART C

MONETARY MANAGEMENT
AND INTEREST RATE TRENDS: SWITZERLAND

NARROWLY DEFINED MONEY SUPPLY (M1)

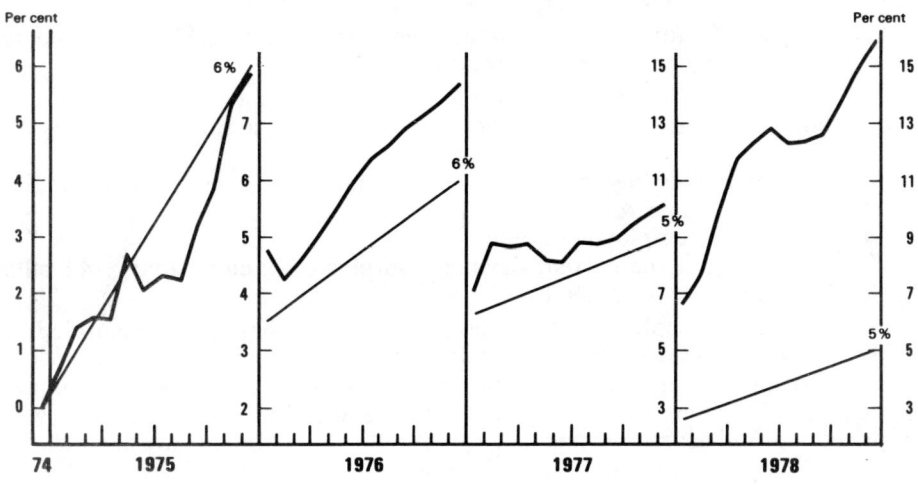

INTEREST RATES

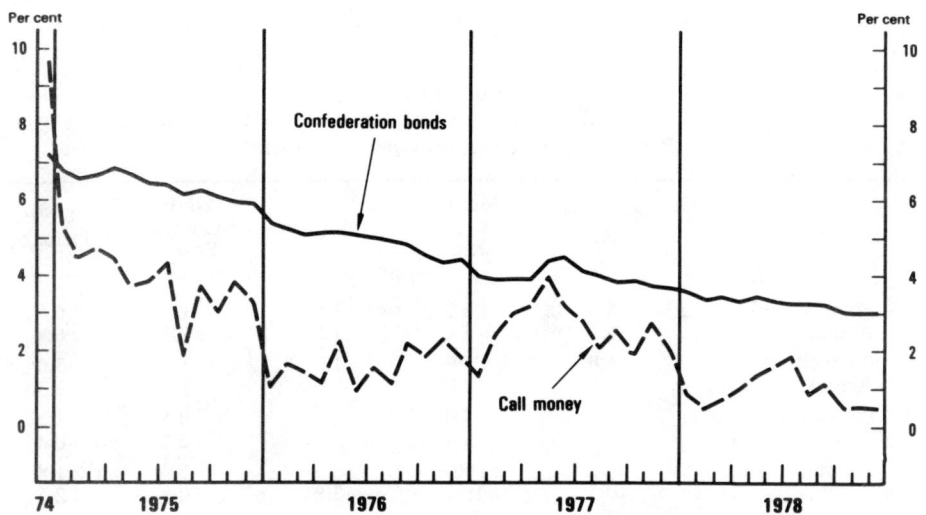

Note: The target for the money supply is expressed as a growth rate over twelve months in 1975 and in terms of annual average growth rates for subsequent years. Straight lines indicate the projected "nominal" growth path for the money stock and are compared with the actual outcome calculated for 1975 as percentage changes relative to the base month, and for 1976, 1977 and 1978 as percentage changes of cumulative monthly averages over the previous year (seasonally adjusted figures).

Short-term interest rates shown in the lower panel largely reflect the authorities' short-run operating strategy in the money market which—together with short-run control of the monetary base—is geared towards the achievement of the intermediate monetary target.

Sources for money supply (seasonally adjusted) and interest rates series: OECD and Morgan Guaranty Trust.

authorities had to cope with considerable capital inflows that tended to boost the Swiss franc's appreciation. These external disturbances explain, to some extent, the divergent trends of the monetary base and M1, and hence the instability of the "multiplier" defined as the ratio between the changes in these two aggregates (Table A).

Comparison of monetary performance with the results achieved in the real economy requires recognition of the following trends:

a) a fall in production in 1975 and 1976, followed by an upturn in 1977, both more marked than anticipated, and then a slow growth in 1978 (Table A);

b) an appreciable decline in the rate of inflation, steeper than had been expected (Table A);

c) a big fall in employment, and

d) a widening of the current payments surplus (to a cumulated $14½ billion between 1975 and 1978).

The role of monetary policy in these developments can hardly be quantified. It must be stressed, however, that the task of the Swiss monetary authorities has been made comparatively easy by a number of factors. An important influence has been the discipline observed by trade unions and firms with regard to wages and prices. Another factor has been the return of foreign workers to their home countries. In addition, there has been the positive effects on domestic prices of the Swiss franc's appreciation which, in effective terms, has amounted to 41 per cent over the past four years, more than would be justified by inflation differentials alone. Finally, the Swiss National Bank enjoys a high degree of independence and respect in the context of overall economic policy-making.

Table A. SWITZERLAND:
MONETARY AGGREGATES, OUTPUT AND PRICES
Percentage increases over previous year

	Monetary Base[a]	Money Supply M1[a]	Multiplier[b]	GNP at Constant Prices	GNP Deflator
1975 - Planned	6.0	6.0	1.5	−1.2	6.5
- Actual	6.2	5.9	1.5	−7.7	6.8
1976 - Planned	6.0	6.0	1.7	1.3	3.0
- Actual	3.8	8.0	3.5	−1.3	2.3
1977 - Planned	..	5.0	..	0.5	1.3
- Actual	5.4	5.4	1.9	2.7	0.4
1978 - Planned	..	5.0	..	2.0	1.8
- Actual	10.5	16.2	2.8	0.9	2.7

a) Growth rates are on end-year basis in 1975 and on yearly average basis in 1976, 1977 and 1978.
b) Ratio of absolute change in M1 to absolute change in monetary base.
Sources: Swiss National Bank and OECD Economic Surveys.

BELGIUM

The primary aims of monetary policy as seen by the authorities have been to stabilise the domestic economy, and to ensure the financing of the government's borrowing requirements, while observing external constraints. To achieve their objectives, the monetary authorities have not focused their attention on individual monetary aggregates, but rather attempted, according to the circumstances, either to influence interest rates or to control domestic credit, in particular to firms and households. Given the presumed close substitutability among various financial assets, the quantity of money has not been given special attention, and the authorities have mainly focused on developments in the financial positions of the different economic sectors.

A variety of instruments has been employed to exercise effective control over the global distribution of credit. By changing its lending rates the central bank can influence the cost of credit and thus, the demand for funds from firms and households. Likewise, the government may use both interest subsidies and controls on mortgage and consumer credit to affect borrowing conditions. The supply of credit has been limited directly by the imposition of credit ceilings and indirectly by control of the lending capacity of financial institutions. The latter has mainly taken the form of restrictions on the refinancing possibilities with the central bank (rediscount quotas, quotas on advances against collateral), reserve requirements and limitations on the banks' access to foreign borrowing. In addition, in the context of public sector financing, financial institutions have on several occasions been required to hold minimum amounts of government securities and/or to allocate part of their new ressources to such holdings. Therefore, it is not possible to identify one single transmission mechanism through which monetary

Table B. BELGIUM: SELECTED FINANCIAL AND GENERAL ECONOMIC INDICATORS

	1970	1971	1972	1973	1974	1975	1976	1977	1978
	Percentage changes during year								
Money Stock M1	6.9	10.0	15.2	7.4	6.2	15.8	6.8	9.5	6.2
M2	7.6	11.6	16.1	14.5	9.4	14.8	13.0	9.0	7.8
Domestic Credit	7.3	10.0	17.7	18.2	9.6	13.4	16.8	13.4	11.2
	Per cent, monthly average								
Call Money Rate	6.3	3.7	2.5	4.8	9.3	4.6	8.4	5.6	6.3
Government Bond Yield	5.6	5.3	7.0	7.4	8.6	8.5	9.1	8.8	8.8
	Per cent of GNP								
Financial Balances									
Government Sector	−3.8	−3.8	−5.0	−4.1	−4.0	−5.8	−6.6	−7.0	−7.2
Individuals and Enterprise Sectors	7.5	7.1	9.1	6.3	5.4	7.3	7.5	6.7	7.2
Foreign Sector	−2.1	−2.2	−3.7	−2.2	−0.7	−0.4	—	0.9	0.7
	U.S. $ million								
Current Balance	736	708	1 357	1 243	647	250	−43	−726	−573
Change in foreign exchange reserves	464	403	386	940	331	516	−590	611	−429
	Percentage changes over previous year								
Real GNP	6.5	4.2	6.0	6.4	4.9	−2.0	5.8	1.2	1.6
Implicit GNP Deflator	4.6	5.2	5.5	6.7	12.2	12.7	7.7	6.8	4.7
	Per cent of total labour force								
Unemployment Rate	1.8	1.7	2.2	2.2	2.4	4.2	5.6	6.3	6.8

Source: Belgium National Bank and Morgan Guaranty Trust.

management has operated; both interest rates and credit availability have played an important role in this respect at one time or another.

While pursuing, in principle, a stable exchange rate policy based on participation in the European currency arrangements, the authorities have resorted to various techniques in order to shield the domestic economy from external disturbances. One element has been the operating of a dual exchange market. In addition, the monetary authorities have been forced to seek increased insulation from international capital flows through other measures.[6] Persistent and growing public sector deficits have in recent years complicated the task of the monetary authorities. Another important development has been the process of despecialisation of financial intermediaries to which the authorities have reacted by submitting non-bank financial institutions to the same set of regulations as commercial banks.

DENMARK

The financing of a large current account deficit has been an essential task assigned to monetary management. The authorities have attempted to accomplish this objective through a high-interest rate policy. Monetary management has thus aimed at maintaining the level of domestic interest rates significantly above those in international capital markets, and ceilings on bank and mortgage institutions lending commitments in conjunction with capital controls have been used as quantitative instruments. Until 1973-1974, the underlying financial balance of the public sector was positive and the banking sector was heavily indebted to the central bank. In these circumstances the central bank had ample scope for controlling bank liquidity. However, commercial banks had easy access to refinancing schemes, they varied the extent to which the ceiling on commitments was actually utilised, and the existence of ceilings on bank loans occasionally induced banks to acquire large quantities of bonds issued by mortgage institutions. Consistent control of monetary conditions was therefore difficult already before the onset of world economic recession, since domestic credit ceilings were not fully operative and capital inflows affected growth of the money supply. Nevertheless, the current account deficit was generally financed without problems before 1974 through a policy of high interest rates.

The recession of 1974-1975 created serious difficulties for monetary management, primarily because of the large swing into deficit of the public sector's financial balance. The government solved its financing problems to a large extent by initially drawing down its balances accumulated at the central bank and later by borrowing from the central bank. Since market interest rates were already high in 1974, the Danish Parliament was hesitant to authorise issues of government bonds out of fears that the long-term bond rate could rise to excessive levels in 1975. At the same time, the link between short and medium-term bank lending rates and the discount rate had loosened, following the breakdown of the General Deposit Interest Rate Agreement in 1973. The central bank therefore introduced a number of new instruments, such as limits on bank borrowing from the central bank, cash reserve requirements on banks, issues of deposit certificates which could not be resold before maturity, and quantitative ceilings on mortgage credit. Limited issues of government bonds

---

6. Four lines of action have been followed in this respect: direct controls have been introduced on banks' external positions; limitations have been imposed on interest paid on non-residents deposits; a partial sterilisation policy has been implemented by the central bank; and the two-tier exchange market system has been managed more strictly. Moreover, the monetary authorities have tended to raise the cost of building up speculative positions through action on interest rates and credit availability.

were authorised. In spite of these measures domestic credit expansion surged in both 1975 and 1976, and private capital imports fell sharply. This development came about following a significant increase in the utilisation rate of authorised bank lending commitments, partly related to disturbances in exchange markets. A sharp rise in the current account deficit in 1976 (to 5 per cent of GDP), resulting from a policy-induced consumer spending surge, had to be covered by massive public borrowing abroad.[7]

Table C. DENMARK: SELECTED FINANCIAL AND GENERAL ECONOMIC INDICATORS

	1970	1971	1972	1973	1974	1975	1976	1977	1978
Percentage changes during year									
Money Stock M1	−2.0	8.5	17.0	10.2	5.8	26.4	6.1	9.0	15.9
M2	2.9	8.8	15.0	12.7	8.9	25.5	11.3	9.8	6.7
Commercial Bank Lending	5.1	3.5	11.5	14.5	7.6	0.4	19.5	12.6	11.7
Circulating Bonds (nominal value)	14.6	16.6	17.1	20.0	19.0	20.5	18.9	17.8	18.8
Per cent, end of period									
Drawings against commercial bank loan commitments	..	..	..	73.1	76.2	70.3	79.1	82.3	83.1
Average Domestic Bond Yield	11.5	11.2	11.2	13.8	14.5	12.7	15.6	16.8	17.4
International Bond Yield[a]	8.1	7.8	7.6	8.3	9.4	8.5	7.4	8.0	8.6
Per cent of GDP									
Current Balance	−3.5	−2.5	−0.3	−1.7	−3.0	−1.4	−5.0	−3.9	−2.6
Change in foreign exchange reserves	—	0.6	0.8	1.2	−0.4	−1.0	0.1	2.3	1.3
Central government financial balance[b]	—	2.9	0.8	1.4	3.0	−0.2	−4.0	−2.3	−2.2
Percentage changes over previous year									
Real GDP	2.7	3.6	4.3	2.8	−0.9	−0.4	7.0	1.9	1.0
Implicit GDP Deflator	7.7	6.2	8.6	10.3	12.5	11.6	7.9	9.2	9.6
Per cent of total labour force									
Unemployment Rate	..	..	..	1.1	2.5	6.0	6.1	7.7	8.8

a) Long-term issues by United States companies in U.S. dollars.
b) Budget basis; balance on current, investment and lending accounts; financial year ending March.
Sources: Danish National Bank and Morgan Guaranty Trust.

From the end of 1976, following a realignment within the EEC "snake", money and credit expansion finally slowed down. This moderation was due to a combination of factors including tight credit policy, a marked shift in the structure of interest rates facilitating large issues of public short- and medium-term bonds, and decelerating growth of real demand subsequent to a renewed

7. The public sector's borrowings in international capital markets were undertaken exclusively under external financing considerations. The loan proceeds were therefore deposited directly with the central bank without any impact on domestic money supply.

tightening of fiscal policy in August 1976. While short- and medium-term interest rates rose sharply, there seems to have been some success in "insulating" the politically sensitive long-term mortgage bond rate. Moreover, government bonds are now mainly being purchased by the non-financial sector rather than the banking system. As a consequence, net private capital inflows rose significantly and in 1977 covered about 75 per cent of the current account deficit. As public borrowing abroad continued at a high rate, there was a large increase in foreign reserves. The balance of payments financing goal of monetary policy thus seems to have been achieved in the most recent period, following the introduction of more efficient policy instruments. But success on the monetary and external front has clearly been at the expense of a continuing widening of nominal and real interest rate differentials between the Danish and international capital markets. This does not seem to have hampered industrial investment activity since Danish enterprises have a large access to international capital markets. However, there seems to be growing public recognition that monetary policy in Denmark may have been somewhat "overworked".[8]

---

8. See E. Hoffmayer and L. Hansen "Danish Monetary Policy During The Last Decade" *Kredit und Kapital,* 1978, No. 2.

Annex III

SELECTED BIBLIOGRAPHY

The following small selection from the current literature includes contributions which, among other sources, served as a basis for the present study. Moreover, the references cited, which necessarily reflect a certain degree of eclecticism, may help the reader to examine some of the topics dealt with in this study in greater depth.

A. CONCEPTUAL AND QUANTITATIVE BASIS OF MONETARY TARGETING

Evaluations of the usefulness of monetary targets by officials of central banks or by international organisations have constituted an important part of the ongoing discussion. Examples of the former include the collection of papers published by the Federal Reserve Banks of Boston (1972) and of New York (1974)[1], the study by the Bank of Japan (1975), and various contributions by economists from the Bank of England, notably Goodhart and Crockett (1970) and Goodhart (1975). Contributions by international organisations include those of the Bank for International Settlements (1976), the Commission of the European Communities (1976), and the International Monetary Fund (1977). A favourable view of targeting also is contained in paragraphs 309-319 of the "McCracken Report" to the OECD (McCracken et al., 1977).

Academic discussion of monetary targeting originated with the "monetarist" school, and the public probably still tends to associate targeting with that approach. One may refer to such recent articles as Pringle (1978) and "All Monetarists Now?" (1977). A thorough review of the development of that approach may be found in Mayer et al. (1978). Other views on the nature of monetarist thought include Stein (1976), Modigliani (1977) and Boughton (1978). In addition to the basic view of the central position of money in macroeconomic theory, monetarism has engendered a number of related concepts such as the "rationality" of price and interest-rate expectations in the aggregate and the dominance of monetary linkages in balance-of-payments adjustment. The development of rational expectations is reviewed in Schiller (1978); and Laidler (1978) discusses different versions of the hypothesis and their relevance to the transmission of monetary policy. Whitman (1975) surveys the concept of global" monetarism. That approach appears to be most relevant to open economies with well developed capital markets; see Neumann (1978) for an example and review. Recent policy positions by prominent members of the monetarist school include notably Carlson (1978) and the reports of the "Shadow European Economic Policy Committee" (1977, 1978).

---

1. Full bibliographical information may be found in the reference list that follows.

Monetary targeting has been subjected to numerous studies in the context of other schools of thought as well. For a general survey of recent monetary theory, see Barro and Fischer (1976). The "Keynesian" school is generally thought to oppose the strict application of targeting, though most economists now recognize the importance of money in the original Keynesian structure. For an evaluation of the role of money in Keynes' thought, see Leijonhufvud (1968), Hicks (1974), and Patinkin (1976). Another view that has played an important part in the discussion might be loosely referred to as the "portfolio-balance" approach. This group includes the "Yale school", a collection of economists including James Tobin at Yale University who have published a number of works arguing that in theory the role of money does not differ qualitatively from that of other financial assets; for a seminal contribution, see Tobin (1971). Related positions have been taken in earlier postwar discussion by Gurley and Shaw (1960) and, in the United Kingdom, by the Committee on the Working of the Monetary System ("Radcliffe Report" 1959). The "New Cambridge" approach has been described in Cripps and Godley (1976). An implication of the portfolio approach is that monetary policy works primarily through its influence on the valuation of capital services in investment markets. For a recent statement in support of that view, see the Council of Economic Advisers (1978), p. 91. Recent econometric work, however, has not corroborated this proposition; see Furstenberg (1977). A reappraisal of the complementary role of portfolio models in monetary policy may be found in Dudler and Chouraqui (1978).

Much of the discussion of targeting techniques has developed in the context of control-theoretic approaches to the problem of policy formation. An early example was the model presented by Mundell (1962) to suggest appropriate roles for monetary and fiscal policy in situations where they were implemented independently; Stern (1973) contains a useful analysis of the Mundell model. Poole (1970) shifted the emphasis to policy-making under uncertainty by arguing that the ability of the authorities to stabilise the economy via control of monetary aggregates depended critically on the relative stability of monetary as opposed to real functional relationships in a neo-Keynesian framework. Benjamin Friedman (1975, 1977) has demonstrated the potential weaknesses of monetary aggregates control, but does not take account of its pragmatic implementation in current monetary management. More theoretical discussions of the technical control problem facing the monetary authorities may be found in Pindyck and Roberts (1974), Craine et al. (1976), Chow (1976) and Turnovsky (1977). Empirical studies of the stability of interest-rate linkages to the real economy are summarized for the United States and the United Kingdom in Savage (1978); see also Furstenberg (1977). Boughton (1979) reviews the evidence on the stability of money demand relationships in several countries.

The effectiveness of monetary policy in the context of overall demand management has been the subject of several strands of academic thought. The role of monetary policy in the inflationary process has been surveyed by Frisch (1977), and the linkages between monetary policy, inflation and employment by Gordon (1976, 1977). A related problem is the appropriate relationship between monetary policy and budgetary and incomes policies. The recent literature on policy coordination and accommodation and the scope for discretionary demand management includes notably Stevenson and Trevithick (1977), Weizsäcker (1977), Fromm and Klein (1976), Modigliani (1977) and Modigliani and Steindel (1977). For a detailed discussion of the desirability of coordination of national monetary policies among countries, see Mathieson (1978) and Thygesen (1977).

BIBLIOGRAPHICAL REFERENCES

"All Monetarists Now?", *The Economist,* 2nd July 1977, pp. 73 f.

Bank for International Settlements, *Forty-sixth Annual Report,* Basle, June 1976, pp. 133 f.

Bank of Japan, "Role of the Money Supply in the Japanese Economy", *Special Paper No. 60,* October 1975.

Barro, Robert and Stanley Fischer, "Recent Developments in Monetary Theory", *Journal of Monetary Economics* No. 2 (1976) esp. pp. 151-155.

Boughton, James M., "The Demand for Money in Major OECD Countries", *OECD Economic Outlook, Occasional Studies,* January 1979.

Boughton, James M., "Does Monetarism Matter?" in Elmus R. Wicker (ed): *Proceedings of the Lilly Conference on Recent Developments in Economics,* Indiana University Press 1978.

Carlson, Keith M., "Does the St. Louis Equation Now Believe in Fiscal Policy?", *Federal Reserve Bank of St. Louis Review,* Vol. 60, No. 2, February 1978, pp. 13-19.

Chow, Gregory C., "Usefulness of Imperfect Models for the Formulation of Stabilisation Policies", Paper presented at the *NBER Conference on Stochastic Control Palo Alto (Calif.),* May 1976.

Commission of the European Communities, *Annual Report on the Economic Situation in the Community,* October 1976, p. 11.

Committee on the Working of the Monetary System: Report, Cmnd. 827, London, August 1959.

Council of Economic Advisers, *Annual Report,* U.S. Government, 1978.

Craine, Roger, Arthur Havenner, James Berry, "Fixed Rules versus Activism in the Conduct of Monetary Policy", *American Economic Review,* December 1978, pp. 769-783.

Cripps, Francis and Wynne Godley, "A Formal Analysis of the Cambridge Economic Policy Group Model", *Economica* 43, November 1976, 335-348.

Dudler, Hermann J. and Jean-Claude Chouraqui, "Flow-of-Funds Analysis in a Short-term Context", *Banque de France, Cahiers Economiques et Monétaires,* No. 7, Paris, 1978.

Federal Reserve Bank of Boston, "Controlling Monetary Aggregates II: The Implementation", Conference Series No. 9, Boston 1972.

Federal Reserve Bank of New York, *Monetary Aggregates and Monetary Policy,* New York 1974.

Friedman, Benjamin, "Targets, Instruments, and Indicators of Monetary Policy", *Journal of Monetary Economics* 1 (1975), pp. 443-473.

Friedman, Benjamin, "The Inefficiency of Short-Run Monetary Targets for Monetary Policy", *Brookings Papers on Economic Activity,* No. 2, 1977, pp. 293-335.

Frisch, Helmut, "Inflation Theory 1963-1975, A Second Generation Survey", *Journal of Economic Literature,* December 1977, pp. 1289-1317.

Fromm, G. and L.R. Klein, "The NBER/NSF Model Comparison Seminar: An Analysis of Results", *Annals of Economic and Social Measurement,* Winter 1976.

Fürstenberg, George M. von, "Corporate Investment: Does Market Valuation Matter in the Aggregate?" in *Brookings Papers on Economic Activity* 2/1977, pp. 247-397.

Goodhart, C.A.E. and A.D. Crockett, "The Importance of Money", *Bank of England Quarterly Bulletin,* Vol. 10, No. 2, June 1970, pp. 159-198.

Goodhart, C.A.E., *Money, Information and Uncertainty,* London 1975.

Gordon, Robert J., "Recent Developments in the Theory of Inflation and Unemployment", *Journal of Monetary Economics*, No. 2 (1966), pp. 185-219.

Gordon, Robert J., "World Inflation and Monetary Accommodation in Eight Countries", *Brookings Papers on Economic Activity*, No. 2/1977, pp. 409-468.

Gurley, J. and E. Shaw, *Money in a Theory of Finance*, Washington, D.C. 1960.

Hicks, John, *The Crisis in Keynesian Economics*, Oxford 1974 (esp. Chapter II).

International Monetary Fund, *The Monetary Approach to the Balance of Payments*, Washington, D.C. 1977.

Laidler, David, "Money and Money Income: An Essay on the 'Transmission Mechanism'", *Journal of Monetary Economics* 4, April 1978, pp. 151-191.

Leijonhufvud, A., *On Keynesian Economics and the Economics of Keynes*, New York 1968.

Mathieson, D.J., "The Coordination of Decentralised Monetary Policies and Exchange Rate Movements: A Theoretical Approach", Banque de France, *Cahiers Economiques et Monétaires*, No. 6, Paris 1978, pp. 257-283.

Mayer, Thomas et al., *The Structure of Monetarism*, New York 1978.

McCracken, Paul et al., *Towards Full Employment and Price Stability*. A report to the OECD by a group of independent experts, Paris, June 1977.

Modigliani, Franco, "The Monetarist Controversy or, Should We Forsake Stabilization Policies?", *American Economic Review*, Vol. 67, No. 2, March 1977, pp. 1-19.

Modigliani, Franco and Charles Steindel, "Is a Tax Rebate an Effective Tool for Stabilisation Policy?", *Brookings Papers on Economic Activity*, 1/1977, pp. 175-209.

Mundell, Robert A., "The Appropriate Use of Monetary and Fiscal Policy for Internal and External Stability", *IMF Staff Papers*, No. 9, March 1962, pp. 70-79.

Neumann, Manfred J.M., "Offsetting Capital Flows", *Journal of Monetary Economics*, No. 4 (1978), pp. 131-142 and the references cited.

Patinkin, Don, *Keynes' Monetary Thought*, Durham, North Carolina, 1976.

Pindyck, Robert S. and Steven M. Roberts, "Optimal Policies for Monetary Control", *Annals of Economic and Social Measurement*, 3/1, 1974, pp. 207-237.

Poole, W., "Optimal Choice of Monetary Policy Instruments in a Simple Stochastic Macro Model", *Quarterly Journal of Economics*, Vol. 84, No. 2, May 1970, pp. 197-216.

Pringle, Robin, "The middle age of monetarism", *The Banker*, April 1978, pp. 31-35.

Savage, David, "The Channels of Monetary Influence: A Survey of Empirical Evidence", *National Institute Economic Review*, No. 83, February 1978, pp. 73-89.

Shadow European Economic Policy Committee" (SEEPC), "Manifestos", Paris, May 27, 1977 and Brussels, 21-31 May, 1978.

Shiller, Robert J., "Rational Expectations and the Dynamic Structure of Macroeconomic Models", *Journal of Monetary Economics*, No. 4 (1978), pp. 1-44.

Stein, Jerome L. (ed), *Monetarism*, Amsterdam 1976.

Stern, Robert M., *The Balance of Payments*, London 1973, Chapter 10.

Stevenson, A.A., and J.A. Trevithick, "The Complementarity of Monetary Policy and Prices and Incomes Policy: An Examination of Recent British Experience", *Scottish Journal of Political Economy*, Vol. 24, No. 1, February 1977, pp. 19-31.

Thygesen, Niels, "International Coordination of Monetary Policies", paper prepared for SUERF Conference on "New Approaches in Monetary Policy" Wiesbaden, Germany, September 29-October 1, 1977.

Tobin, James, *"Essays in Economics, Volume 1, Macroeconomics"*, North Holland Publishing Company, 1971.

Turnovsky, Stephen J., "On the Scope of Optimal and Discretionary Policies in the Stabilisation of Stochastic Linear Systems", in John D. Pitchford and Stephen J. Turnovsky: *Applications of Control Theory to Economic Analysis*, Amsterdam 1977, pp. 337-363.

Weizsäcker, C. Ch. von, "The Employment Problem: A Systems Approach", *Paper presented at Expert Meeting on Structural Determinants of Employment and Unemployment*, OECD Paris, 7-11th March, 1977, pp. 25 ff.

Whitman, Marina v. N., "Global Monetarism and the Monetary Approach to the Balance of Payments", in *Brookings Papers on Economic Activity*, 3/1975, pp. 491-536.

B. COUNTRY EXPERIENCE

Systematic cross-country reviews of experience with monetary targeting are still rare. Most of the contributions cited below refer to sources reviewing recent developments in the field of target-oriented monetary management for individual countries.

CROSS-COUNTRY REFERENCES

Banque de France, Actes du séminaire des Banques Centrales et des Institutions Internationales, Paris, April 1977, Ire partie: "Les instruments et les objectifs de la politique monétaire". *Cahiers Economiques et Monétaires,* No. 6 (1978).

Bank for International Settlements (Basle), *46th Annual Report,* 1976.

Duwendag, Dieter, "The 'New Era' of Controlling Monetary Aggregates: Federal Reserve, Swiss National Bank, German Bundesbank", *Paper prepared for 1977 Konstanz Seminar on Monetary Theory and Monetary Policy* (June 7-10).

McClam, Warren D., "Targets and Techniques of Monetary Policy in Western Europe", *Banca Nazionale del Lavoro Quarterly Review,* March 1978.

SUERF Colloquium Wiesbaden (Germany), September 20th-October 1, 1977, on "New Approaches in Monetary Policy" (Papers and Proceedings published in 1979 by Sijthoff and Noordhoff, the Netherlands).

COUNTRY MONOGRAPHS

UNITED STATES

Axilrod, S.H. "Monetary Aggregates and Money Market Conditions in Open Market Policy", *Federal Reserve Bulletin,* Vol. 57, February 1971, pp. 79-104.

Coldwell, Philip E., "The Supply and Cost of Money as Guides to Monetary Policy", paper presented at *26th Annual UCLA Business Forecasting Conference,* University of California, Los Angeles, December 1977.

Davis, Richard G., "Implementing Open Market Policy with Monetary Aggregate Objectives", in *Monetary Aggregates and Monetary Policy,* Federal Reserve Bank of New York, 1974, pp. 7-19.

Davis, Richard G., "Monetary Objectives and Monetary Policy" *Federal Reserve Bank of New York, Quarterly Review,* spring 1977, pp. 29-36.

Federal Reserve System, Board of Governors, *Annual Report,* Washington, 1975, 1976, 1977.

Lang, Richard W., "The Federal Open Market Committee in 1977", *Federal Reserve Bank of St. Louis, Review,* vol. 60, March 1978, pp. 2-21.

Pierce, James L., "Quantitative Analysis for Decision Making at the Federal Reserve", *Annals of Economic and Social Measurement,* January 1974, pp. 11-19.

Poole, William, "The Making of Monetary Policy: Description and Analysis", *Federal Reserve Bank of Boston, New England Economic Review,* March/April 1975, pp. 21-30.

Thunberg, R., "Monetary Objectives and Monetary Policy in the United States", Banque de France, *Cahiers Economiques et Monétaires,* No. 6, April 1977.

Volcker, Paul A., "The Role of Monetary Targets in an Age of Inflation", *Journal of Monetary Economics* 4:2, April 1978, pp. 329-39.

Wallich Henry C. and Peter M. Keir, "The Role of Operating Guides in U.S. Monetary Policy: A Historical Review", *Kredit und Kapital,* H 11.1, 1978, pp. 30-52.

JAPAN

Bank of Japan, "Role of Money Supply in the Japanese Economy", *Special paper No. 60,* October 1975.

Bank of Japan, "Rising Trend Line of the Marshallian k", *Special paper No. 73,* February 1978.

Komiya, Ryutaro and Yoshio Suzuki, "Inflation in Japan" in *Worldwide Inflation,* edited by L.B. Krause and W.S. Salant, *The Brookings Institution,* 1977.

Quirk, P.J., "Exchange Rate Policy in Japan: Leaning Against the Wind", *IMF Staff Papers,* Vol. XXIV, No. 3, November 1977.

Uehara, H., "Changes in Japan's Flow of Funds and Their Implication for Future Monetary Policy", in *Banque de France, Cahiers Economiques et Monétaires,* No. 7, 1978.

GERMANY

Annual Reports of the Council of Economic Advisers (1974/1975).

Bockelmann, Horst, "Quantitative Targets for Monetary Policy in Germany", in *Banque de France, Cahiers Economiques et Monétaires,* No. 6, 1978.

Duwendag, Dieter, "The 'New Era' of Controlling Monetary Aggregates: Federal Reserve, Swiss National Bank, German Bundesbank", *paper prepared for 1977 Konstanz Seminar on Monetary Theory and Monetary Policy.*

Frowen, S.F., A.S. Courakis and M.H. Miller, *Monetary Policy and Economic Activity in West Germany,* New York 1977.

Hötterhoff, V., "Geldpolitik sollte wieder stetigeren kurs fahren", *Ifo-Institut, Schnelldienst,* 31 jg., May 1978.

Föhler, Claus, *Probleme der Zentralbankgeldmengensteuerung,* Berlin 1976.

Pohl, Rheinhard. "Hat sich die reue geldpolitische Strategie der Deutschen Bundesrepublik bewahrt?", *Deutsches Institut für Wirtschaftsforschung Vierteljahres,* heft, 1/1978, pp. 5-21.

Schlesinger, Helmut, "Problems of Monetary Policy in Germany: Some Basic Issues", *Opening Address at the SUERF Colloquium, Wiesbaden* (Germany), September 29, 1977.

Schlesinger, Helmut, Neuere Erfahreungen der Geldpolitik in der Bundesrepublik Deutschland", *Kredit und Kapital,* 28 Jg. H. 4, 1976.

FRANCE

Banque de France, *Compte rendu annuel,* exercices 1976 et 1977.

Chazelas, M., J.F. Dauvisis and G. Maarek, "L'expérience française d'encadrement du crédit, *Banque de France, Cahiers Economiques et Monétaires,* No. 6, 1978.

Chouraqui, J.C., "Recent Monetary Policy Experience in France" paper presented at *Conference on Recent Developments in Western Economies,* Oxford (Brasenose College), July 1976.

Geniere, R. de la, "Les moyens de la politique monétaire vus de la Banque de France", *Revue Banque,* May 1976.

Pecha, J., "Mise en pratique d'un objectif monétaire en France", *SUERF Colloquium Wiesbaden,* October 1977.

UNITED KINGDOM

Coghlan, R.T., "A Transactions Demand for Money", *Bank of England, Quarterly Bulletin,* Vol. 18, March 1978, pp. 48-60.

Dicks-Mireaux, L.A., "British Monetary Experience, 1973-1977", paper presented at *Eighth Konstanz Seminar on Monetary Theory and Monetary Policy,* June 8-10, 1977.

Goodhart, C.A.E., "Problems of Monetary Management: The United Kingdom Experience", paper presented at *Conference on Recent Developments in Western Economies,* Oxford (Brasenose College), July 1976.

Hewitt, M., "Financial Forecasts in the United Kingdom", *Banque de France, Cahiers Economiques et Monétaires,* No. 7, 1978.

OECD, "Short-run Monetary Management and the Exchange Rate", *Economic Survey: United Kingdom,* Annexe I, Paris, March 1977.

Price, L.D.D., "Monetary Objectives and Instruments in the United Kingdom", *Banque de France, Cahiers Economiques et Monétaires,* No. 6, 1978, pp. 205-218.

Richardson, Gordon, Speech at Lord Mayor's Dinner on 20th October 1977, reproduced in *Bank of England Quarterly Bulletin,* Vol. 17, December 1977, pp. 461-63.

Wass, Douglas, "The Changing Problems of Economic Management", *Economic Trends,* March 1978, pp. 97-104.

ITALY

Banca Commerciale Italiana Quarterly Bulletin, *Monetary Trends,* Nos. 3/4 (1975), 5,7 (1976) 9,10,11 (1978).

Cotula, F. and S. Micossi, "Some Considerations on the Choice of Intermediate Monetary Targets in the Italian economy", *Banque de France, Cahiers Economiques et Monétaires,* No. 6, 1978.

Padoa Schioppa, T., "Selective Credit Policy: Italy's Recent Experience", *Banca Nazionale del Lavoro, Quarterly Review,* March 1975.

Vaciago, G., "Monetary Policy in Italy: the Limited Role of Monetarism", *Banca Nazionale del Lavoro, Quarterly Review,* December 1977.

CANADA

Bouey, Gerald K., "Remarks to the Calgary Chamber of Commerce", in *Bank of Canada Monthly Review,* October 1977.

Courchene, Thomas J., *Monetarism and Control: The Inflation Fighters* (Toronto: C.D. Howe, Research Institute, 1976).

Freeman, George E., "Recent Developments in Canadian Monetary Policy", *Kredit und Kapital,* H. 11.2 (1978), pp. 145-58.

Governor of the Bank of Canada, *Annual Report* (Ottawa: 1975, 1976, 1977).

White, William R., "The Demand for Money in Canada and the Control of the Monetary Aggregates: Evidence from Monthly Data", *Bank of Canada Staff Research Studies,* 1976.

OECD
MONETARY STUDIES SERIES

Also available :

MONETARY POLICY IN JAPAN
1972, 105 pages   US$ 3.50   £ 1.14   F 14,00

MONETARY POLICY IN ITALY
1973, 90 pages   US$ 3.75   £ 1.32   F 15,00

MONETARY POLICY IN GERMANY
1973, 130 pages   US$ 5.25   £ 2.10   F 21,00

MONETARY POLICY IN THE UNITED STATES
1974, 206 pages   US$ 9.50   £ 3.80   F 38,00

MONETARY POLICY IN FRANCE
1974, 108 pages   US$ 5.25   £ 2.10   F 21,00

THE ROLE OF MONETARY POLICY IN DEMAND MANAGEMENT THE EXPERIENCE OF SIX MAJOR COUNTRIES
1975, 148 pages   US$ 6.25   £ 2.80   F 25,00

OECD SALES AGENTS
DÉPOSITAIRES DES PUBLICATIONS DE L'OCDE

ARGENTINA – ARGENTINE
Carlos Hirsch S.R.L., Florida 165, 4° Piso (Galería Guemes)
1333 BUENOS-AIRES, Tel. 33-1787-2391 Y 30-7122

AUSTRALIA – AUSTRALIE
Australia & New Zealand Book Company Pty Ltd.,
23 Cross Street, (P.O.B. 459)
BROOKVALE NSW 2100   Tel. 938-2244

AUSTRIA – AUTRICHE
Gerold and Co., Graben 31, WIEN 1. Tel. 52.22.35

BELGIUM – BELGIQUE
LCLS
44 rue Otlet, B1070 BRUXELLES. Tel. 02-521 28 13

BRAZIL – BRÉSIL
Mestre Jou S.A., Rua Guaipá 518,
Caixa Postal 24090, 05089 SAO PAULO 10. Tel. 261-1920
Rua Senador Dantas 19 s/205-6, RIO DE JANEIRO GB.
Tel. 232-07. 32

CANADA
Renouf Publishing Company Limited,
2182 St. Catherine Street West,
MONTREAL, Quebec H3H 1M7 Tel. (514) 937-3519

DENMARK – DANEMARK
Munksgaards Boghandel,
Nørregade 6, 1165 KØBENHAVN K. Tel. (01) 12 85 70

FINLAND – FINLANDE
Akateeminen Kirjakauppa
Keskuskatu 1, 00100 HELSINKI 10. Tel. 625.901

FRANCE
Bureau des Publications de l'OCDE,
2 rue André-Pascal, 75775 PARIS CEDEX 16. Tel. (1) 524.81.67
Principal correspondant :
13602 AIX-EN-PROVENCE : Librairie de l'Université.
Tel. 26.18.08

GERMANY – ALLEMAGNE
Alexander Horn,
D - 6200 WIESBADEN, Spiegelgasse 9
Tel. (6121) 37-42-12

GREECE – GRÈCE
Librairie Kauffmann, 28 rue du Stade,
ATHÈNES 132. Tel. 322.21.60

HONG-KONG
Government Information Services,
Sales and Publications Office, Beaconsfield House, 1st floor,
Queen's Road, Central.   Tel. 5-233191

ICELAND – ISLANDE
Snaebjörn Jónsson and Co., h.f.,
Hafnarstraeti 4 and 9, P.O.B. 1131, REYKJAVIK.
Tel. 13133/14281/11936

INDIA – INDE
Oxford Book and Stationery Co.:
NEW DELHI, Scindia House. Tel. 45896
CALCUTTA, 17 Park Street. Tel. 240832

ITALY – ITALIE
Libreria Commissionaria Sansoni:
Via Lamarmora 45, 50121 FIRENZE. Tel. 579751
Via Bartolini 29, 20155 MILANO. Tel. 365083
Sub-depositari:
Editrice e Libreria Herder,
Piazza Montecitorio 120, 00 186 ROMA. Tel. 674628
Libreria Hoepli, Via Hoepli 5, 20121 MILANO. Tel. 865446
Libreria Lattes, Via Garibaldi 3, 10122 TORINO. Tel. 519274
La diffusione delle edizioni OCSE è inoltre assicurata dalle migliori
librerie nelle città più importanti.

JAPAN – JAPON
OECD Publications and Information Center
Akasaka Park Building, 2-3-4 Akasaka, Minato-ku,
TOKYO 107. Tel. 586-2016

KOREA - CORÉE
Pan Korea Book Corporation,
P.O.Box n° 101 Kwangwhamun, SÉOUL. Tel. 72-7369

LEBANON – LIBAN
Documenta Scientifica/Redico,
Edison Building, Bliss Street, P.O.Box 5641, BEIRUT.
Tel. 354429—344425

MALAYSIA – MALAISIE
University of Malaya Co-operative Bookshop Ltd.
P.O. Box 1127, Jalan Pantai Baru
Kuala Lumpur, Malaysia. Tel. 51425, 54058, 54361

THE NETHERLANDS – PAYS-BAS
Staatsuitgeverij
Chr. Plantijnstraat
'S-GRAVENHAGE. Tel. 070-814511
Voor bestellingen: Tel. 070-624551

NEW ZEALAND – NOUVELLE-ZÉLANDE
The Publications Manager,
Government Printing Office,
WELLINGTON: Mulgrave Street (Private Bag),
World Trade Centre, Cubacade, Cuba Street,
Rutherford House, Lambton Quay, Tel. 737-320
AUCKLAND: Rutland Street (P.O.Box 5344), Tel. 32.919
CHRISTCHURCH: 130 Oxford Tce (Private Bag), Tel. 50.331
HAMILTON: Barton Street (P.O.Box 857), Tel. 80.103
DUNEDIN: T & G Building, Princes Street (P.O.Box 1104),
Tel. 78.294

NORWAY – NORVÈGE
J.G. Tanum A/S
P.O. Box 1177 Sentrum
Karl Johansgate 43
OSLO 1 Tel (02) 80 12 60

PAKISTAN
Mirza Book Agency, 65 Shahrah Quaid-E-Azam, LAHORE 3.
Tel. 66839

PORTUGAL
Livraria Portugal, Rua do Carmo 70-74,
1117 LISBOA CODEX.
Tel. 360582/3

SPAIN – ESPAGNE
Mundi-Prensa Libros, S.A.
Castelló 37, Apartado 1223, MADRID-1. Tel. 275.46.55
Libreria Bastinos, Pelayo, 52, BARCELONA 1. Tel. 222.06.00

SWEDEN – SUÈDE
AB CE Fritzes Kungl Hovbokhandel,
Box 16 356, S 103 27 STH, Regeringsgatan 12,
DS STOCKHOLM. Tel. 08/23 89 00

SWITZERLAND – SUISSE
Librairie Payot, 6 rue Grenus, 1211 GENÈVE 11. Tel. 022-31.89.50

TAIWAN – FORMOSE
National Book Company,
84-5 Sing Sung Rd., Sec. 3, TAIPEI 107. Tel. 321.0698

THAILAND – THAILANDE
Suksit Siam Co., Ltd.
1715 Rama IV Rd,
Samyan, Bangkok 5
Tel. 2511630

UNITED KINGDOM – ROYAUME-UNI
H.M. Stationery Office, P.O.B. 569,
LONDON SEI 9 NH. Tel. 01-928-6977, Ext. 410 or
49 High Holborn, LONDON WC1V 6 HB (personal callers)
Branches at: EDINBURGH, BIRMINGHAM, BRISTOL,
MANCHESTER, CARDIFF, BELFAST.

UNITED STATES OF AMERICA
OECD Publications and Information Center, Suite 1207,
1750 Pennsylvania Ave., N.W. WASHINGTON, D.C. 20006.
Tel. (202)724-1857

VENEZUELA
Libreria del Este, Avda. F. Miranda 52, Edificio Galipàn,
CARACAS 106. Tel. 32 23 01/33 26 04/33 24 73

YUGOSLAVIA – YOUGOSLAVIE
Jugoslovenska Knjiga, Terazije 27, P.O.B. 36, BEOGRAD.
Tel. 621-992

Les commandes provenant de pays où l'OCDE n'a pas encore désigné de dépositaire peuvent être adressées à :
OCDE, Bureau des Publications, 2 rue André-Pascal, 75775 PARIS CEDEX 16.
Orders and inquiries from countries where sales agents have not yet been appointed may be sent to:
OECD, Publications Office, 2 rue André-Pascal, 75775 PARIS CEDEX 16.

OECD PUBLICATIONS, 2 rue André-Pascal, 75775 Paris Cedex 16 - No. 41 255 1979
PRINTED IN FRANCE
(11 79 05 1) ISBN 92-64-11963-9

LIBRARY OF DAVIDSON COLLEGE

Books on regular loan may be checked out for **two weeks.** Books must be presented at the Circulation Desk in order to be renewed.

A fine is charged after date due.

Special books are subject to special regulations at the the library staff.

FEB -7 198
MAY -7 1990
APR -2